Fraud-Related Interviewing

Fraud-Related Interviewing

Don Rabon

Tanya Chapman

CAROLINA ACADEMIC PRESS

Durham, North Carolina

Library of Congress Cataloging-in-Publication Data

Rabon, Don.
Fraud-related interviewing / Don Rabon, Tanya Chapman.
    p. cm.
ISBN 978-1-59460-706-6 (alk. paper)
1. Fraud investigation. 2. Interviewing. 3. Fraud. I. Chapman,
Tanya. II. Title.

HV8079.F7R33 2010
363.25'4--dc22

                                    2010020099

CAROLINA ACADEMIC PRESS
700 Kent Street
Durham, North Carolina 27701
Telephone (919) 489-7486
Fax (919) 493-5668
www.cap-press.com

Printed in the United States of America

Contents

Preface

How to Utilize This Text

This text was written to address a work in progress. The work in progress is your fraud-related interviewing capabilities and effectiveness. The objective herein is to respond to the diversity of readership interviewing skill levels. On one extreme you are new to the interview process in and of itself and now find yourself responsible for conducting interviews which may include focusing on fraud. You may be an auditor, a newly appointed investigator in the public or private sector, a human resource director, CEO or the like. On the other extreme, you have been conducting fraud-related interviews since the creation and interviews in general well before then. In between the two extremes are the vast majority of readers. You have knowledge, skills and abilities regarding the interview process and are now focusing on fraud-related interviewing specifically and are determined to improve even more.

Our goal is to serve all interviewing skill levels and this text unfolds accordingly. As you proceed through the text you will find:

- **Teaching points:** information applying directly to the conduct of the fraud-related interview.
- **Applications questions:** these are designed to link what is already known with the material presented. You can choose to pass quickly by a given question or pause to reflect, apply and assimilate.
- **Exercises:** these are the "doing" components of the text. Just as there are exercises to increase sports related skills or artis-

tic related skills, herein are exercises designed to enhance interviewing related skills.

- **Chapter Take Away:** The critical interviewing related component within the chapter for chapters one through six.
- **Interviewing Skill Enhancement Activity:** Provides an activity to enhance the related interviewing ability addressed in the chapter. Found in chapters one through six.
- **Quick Interviewing Related Inserts:** Questions, observations or recommendations from others involved in fraud-related interviewing. These inserts are designed to provide a salient interviewing element or to make the reader think upon the question asked or the observation provided as they read the related information in the chapter.
- **Examinations:** found at the end of chapters one through seven.

Please note this text is **designed to focus on the dynamics of the fraud-related interview specifically.** Consequently, for those also seeking additional information regarding the foundations of the interview process to include questioning, detecting deception and persuasion, we would reference you to the following texts. These additional resources can serve to provide the opportunity for further study as relating to your particular interviewing responsibilities.

> **Interviewing and Interrogation** 2nd Edition, Rabon, Chapman, Carolina Academic Press;
> **Persuasive Interviewing** (text and **Participant Workbook**), Rabon, Chapman, Carolina Academic Press;
> **Investigative Discourse Analysis**, Rabon, Carolina Academic Press.

The website for Carolina Academic Press is **www.cap-press.com**.

Wherever you may find yourself vis-à-vis the skill level necessary to conduct fraud-related interviews, this text is designed to take you from where you are to where you would like to be. As with most things in life you will get out of this text what you invest into processing the information, intensely addressing the questions and meticulously performing the exercises. A cursory reading of this text will result in correlating benefits. A slow, deliberate work through of the material will broaden the interviewer's perspective and provide additional options for responding to the ever changing dynamic within the conduct of a fraud-related interview.

The text unfolds as follows: The foundational component will consist of the presentation, analysis and amplification of an interview conducted with a convicted fraudster. Within the interview the interviewee will relate the precipitating circumstances relating to his personal fraud, his fraud methodologies and situational outcomes in response to the inquiries of the interviewer. He will relate his activities while referencing to Company A and Company B.

As the interview with the fraudster unfolds:

- Appropriate application questions will be posed to the reader. These questions are designed to link the reader to the information provided and to expand his/her understanding of the dynamics regarding the commission of fraud and their subsequent relation to the conduct of the fraud-related interview;
- Explanations are provided that address fraud-related interviewing applications;
- Appropriate exercises.

All of the text elements are designed to assist in transitioning the reader from his/her current level (as they define it) of fraud-related interviewing to the skill level to which they aspire.

The questions asked and communication devices utilized by the interviewer should be examined carefully. They are structured to serve as questioning reference examples and interviewing techniques in the reader's own subsequent fraud-related interviews as well as operating within the context of the interview.

Additionally, the text incorporates the information provided by another convicted fraudster regarding his cognitions before and during the commission of the fraud, efforts to avoid detection and mindsets during the conduct of the interview.

Lastly, you will find the further you progress in the text the more challenging the application questions and the exercises become. They should prove to be informative challenges and interesting explorations to those intrepid pilgrims seeking to improve their fraud-related interviewing abilities. Toward that end they will inevitably cause the reader to struggle. Remember however, that the learning is in the struggle.

Feedback, questions, shared experiences and observations from the "field" are always appreciated. We can be reached at dwrabon@msn.com and te.chapman@hotmail.com.

Introduction

Fraud, with its endless variety of manifestations, has been around for a long time. For example, in the first century a startup organization was created. Two of its members—a husband and wife—decided to retain an amount of organizational funds for themselves. Following this, a brief but thorough investigation was undertaken, which and it involved conducting interviews with the targets of the investigation. In each case, deception on the part of the interviewee was involved. The organization had a strong, no-tolerance policy with regard to fraud. As a result, both fraudsters were dead within three hours. Like any organization, the internal grapevine was operating at full capacity and word of what had happened quickly percolated throughout its members. As would be expected, this incident quickly got everyone's attention and generated a great deal of respect for and fear of the consequences for violating the organizational fraud policy. It is assumed that the reduced fraud incidents reflected the newfound respect, for some period of time thereafter, among members of the organization.

The organization was the newly formed and developing Christian church. The fraud-related interviews were conducted by Simon Peter ("Simon" means "hearing," an excellent attribute for any interviewer) Peter. As in any case of fraud there was concealment and deceit. A full account can be found in Acts, 5:1–11.

A good deal of time has passed since this act of fraud occurred, but not much has changed. Fraud is evidenced on all levels of human endeavor—federal, state, local, private and public sectors, occupational, secular and spiritual organizations, national and international. It is impossible to read or watch the news and not be confronted with yet more incidents involving fraud. Today, as we finalize this text, there are reports of a significant embezzlement case in a major city involving the public school system. Among those charged are two principals. The prosecutor referenced a "culture of corruption."

An audit revealed there was $2.1 million misappropriated annually, including unauthorized healthcare payments, cell phones, and motorcycles. Fraud manipulations can range from the individual who embezzles money from the charity fund of the local women's league to the head of a multinational corporation making false statements on the annual report, to an individual who steals classified information and exchanges it for money with a foreign country.

Prosecuting Fraud

One of the major challenges in the fight against fraud is the prosecution thereof. Fraud can, and often does, involve a complexity of undertakings on the part of the fraudster. Consequently, it is a daunting task for the prosecution explaining those complexities to twelve people who could not manage to avoid jury duty. Often the case is prosecuted by a newer assistant district attorney with limited trial experience who does not possess an abundant knowledge of the financial complexities involved in many fraud cases and this may result in the blind leading the blind.

Finally, and potentially the most debilitating to the successful prosecution, is the inadvertent creation of a sympathetic jury during the conduct of the trial. Adding these three dynamics together, it is easy to see why prosecutors are often reluctant to take a fraud case to trial. Here is fraud reality 101: the investigation or audit can produce a preponderance of evidence but no admission of guilt; the prosecution may be unwilling to take the case and may therefore be open to the prospect of allowing the fraudster to plea bargain.

Conversely, the case may not have involved a great deal of evidence initially but *an admission was obtained!* In this case, the prosecution would be much more receptive to taking the case forward.

The fraud-related interview as an admission—seeking vehicle is a fundamental focus of this text.

This text concerns itself with the interview process as it relates to the fraud investigation, a fraud-related audit, or inquiry into a reported fraud. Our position is that the dynamics of fraud itself are inexorably connected to the subsequent fraud interview and ultimately the outcome of the investigation. The interview is not an isolated event but rather a part of the *nagare*, (a Japanese word meaning "flow") of the entire (in this case) fraud dynamic from precursors, to the commission of the crime, to closure. In the fraud-related interview, the interviewer connects three different time periods—the past, the present, and the future. The past addresses the dynamics of the individual and his or her subsequent behavior resulting in the commission of the fraud. The future is the sought after successful outcome of the fraud investigation. The present involves the conduct of the interview itself. In the present, the interviewer seeks to connect the past and the future—the flow, if you will, of all three.

Like Shakespeare's Hamlet, the complexities of mind and motive make fraud-related interviewing one of the most challenging and intellectually exciting of the various crime-specific interview dynamics. As we examine together these complexities, our twofold purpose in developing this text is to enhance the interviewer's knowledge, skill, and abilities in the fraud-related interview and, just as importantly, to open the interviewer's mind to the idea: *What a piece of work is man! how noble in reason! how infinite in faculty! in form and moving how express and admirable! in action how like an angel! in apprehension how like a god! the beauty of the world, the paragon of animals!* (*Hamlet* act II, scene II).

If you have an interest in exploring the fraudster as, indeed, a most fascinating and challenging "piece of work," then now in your hands is the right text. Let's get going.

Fraud-Related
Interviewing

Chapter 1

Before We Get Started

What do you do to prepare yourself for a fraud-related interview?

- *Organize information for interview.*
- *Determine whom you will have to interview.*
- *Review questions and documentation for interview.*

Inquiries 1 to 3

Application Question 1: What effect, if any, do you believe the initial moments of the fraud-related interview plays in the overall conduct and ultimate success of the interview?

Application Question 2: What preparation do you give toward the first few moments of the interview?

Application Question 3: Have you ever conducted an interview wherein you could tell from the first few moments the interview would go well? How did you know?

Application Question 4: Have you ever conducted an interview wherein you could tell from the first few moments the interview would go poorly? How did you know?

Application Question 5: If someone were to ask you to tell them about yourself, how would you describe yourself?

Starting the Fraud-Related Interview

I find the introductory phase of an interview to be the most difficult. During this time, I am establishing rapport, trying to get a read on the subject, and determine the best approach to obtain the information needed.

—Anonymous class participant

Inquiries 1 to 3

Interviewing Inquiry 1

Interviewer: David, before we get started, if you will tell me about yourself.

> **Teaching Point:** As with any interview, the initiation of the fraud-related interview is a most critical phase. Certainly, whatever legal or organizational prerequisites that have been established must be followed. Having accomplished those criteria, the opening gambit found in the question above merits explanation and consideration. Consider the following: the author's approach is to have the (literal) table clear. The goal is to establish the social framework of two people simply talking. Quickly showing the interviewee the palms of your hands, calling him or her by name and saying, "before we get started, if you will tell me about yourself" is a most viable option for opening the interview.
>
> Calling the interviewee by name will grab and focus the interviewee's attention. Showing the palms of the hands indicates honesty and openness. The words, "before we get started" serve to indicate to the interviewee that the interview has not started yet. There is no reason to raise the interviewee's shields or move him or her to the *en garde* position. The usage of the collective pronoun "we" is designed to engender a sense of having already established a cooperative relationship. The pronoun "you" tends to involve either explicitly or implicitly a finger-pointing connotation and its use should be limited.

Subject: Basically, I was raised, was born in Winston-Salem, North Carolina, but my family moved when I was like six years old to Charleston, South Carolina. So that's been where I was basically raised. Of course my mom and dad are still living. I've got two siblings that are still living. I have children. They all still live there in Winston. I went to high school in Winston-Salem. Graduated from high school. Went to a local community college one year. Met my wife, my first wife, Marie at the community college. We transferred after that first year to the University of North Carolina. Where she got her business management degree and I got a degree in finance. From there I've got four children, Mary, Susan, Helen, and Sandra. They live with their mother still in Winston-Salem. And that is a quick version of who I am and where I'm from.

Application Question 6: In the above response how did the interviewee describe himself?

Application Question 7: Who was mentioned in the description?

Application Question 8: How were the relationships articulated?

Application Question 9: From his overall self-description what impression do you have?

Application Question 10: What is revealed by the key phrase "a quick version of who I am" in the last sentence of the interviewee's self-description?

Discovering the Interviewee

Teaching Point: Having employed the opening strategy and asked the opening question, pay attention to how the interviewee describes himself or herself and whether the individual is willing to share self-descriptive information.

People display what is important to them in their offices and homes. Examples of what are is important include symbols, pictures of family members, diplomas, awards, emblems, team clothing, or memorabilia. Likewise interviewees will, under the appropriate guidance from the interviewer, provide insight into themselves through their self-descriptions. The goal is to ascertain how the interviewee describes himself right at that point in his/her life. The interviewer should always be thinking, "Of all the choices that this person has with regard to describing themselves, at this point they have chosen this criteria to self-describe." How the interviewee chooses to self-describe can provide insight into his or her current cognitions as well as provide possible connections into any motivations relative to the commission of fraud. The interviewer seeks to evaluate any connections that link how the interviewee articulates himself and the reason for the interview, as well as listen for some descriptive element he/she can relate to in order to establish a connection with the interviewee. For example, an interviewee may describe himself as follows: "Well right now I am taking care of my mother. She has been ill for the last several months and I am trying to help her get through this medical and financial crisis. I have sublet my apartment and moved in with her to watch over her and offset some of her expenses." Certainly, in a fraud-related interview the interviewer should be giving thought as to the possibility that the interviewee's newly experienced financial pressure/motive (more about that in a bit) may be linked to the reason for the inquiry.

Interviewing Inquiry 2

Interviewer: Where is Charleston in relationship to Greenville?

Subject: To Greenville? Greenville is in the northwest corner. It's actually a drive of several hours if you take the interstate route from Charleston.

Interviewing Inquiry 3

Interviewer: I've been to Charleston and also to Winston-Salem a number of times.

Subject: Okay.

Sharing Something about Yourself

Teaching Point: Once the individual has laid some self-descriptive cards about themselves on the table, the interviewer should respond with some related elements about themselves. Notice in the last exchange the interviewer has shared with the interviewee that he had visited both of the cities the interviewee had mentioned "a number of times." Never forget people (the interviewee in this case) respond to people (the interviewer) who respond to them. If, however, the interviewee should respond with, "What do you need to know about me for?" or "What has that got to do with anything?" simply respond with, "Okay, let's get right to the point," and transition into the continuation of the interview.

Read the following opening self-description from another person convicted of fraud.

Subject: I was born and raised in Atlanta, Georgia. Grew up there. My family was probably as dysfunctional as they come and I don't want to brag about that. My parents were divorced when I was three years old. My mother was having medical problems. I lived with my father. I had an older brother and two older sisters. I was kind of the baby of the family. My next youngest sister was nine years older than I was. I guess I realized that ... back in the beginning when I was born or maybe five, six, seven years old that I had the ability to talk my way out of things ... a knack for ... a knack ... I use that word *knack*. A knack for being able to talk my way out of anything. If I ever got in trouble in school—if I ever got in trouble with my grandparents—I was always able to talk my way out of it. It was kind of tough growing up. My father was in the bakery business. My grandfather was in the bakery business. They really didn't get along too well. Unfortunately I was in the middle. So that basically ... I guess you would say that I came from a broken home.

Application Question 11: In what context regarding others does the interviewee describe himself?

Application Question 12: What interview strategy adjustments, if any, would you undertake, when the interviewee articulates he has learned he has the ability "to talk my way out of anything"?

Application Question 13: What would be your connecting response to this interviewee as it applies to Question 12: above?

Application Question 14: What are the salient points raised in the interviewee's description of himself?

Application Question 15: How would you formulate a question with regard to his mother's medical problems?

Application Question 16: How would you formulate a question with regard to the divorce of his parents?

Application Question 17: How would you formulate a question with regard to his siblings?

Application Question 18: How would you formulate a question with regard to the conflict between his father and grandfather and his being caught in the middle?

Application Question 19: How would you formulate a question with regard to his description of his family as dysfunctional?

Application Question 20: Why would Application Questions 14–18 be appropriate at this stage of the interview process?

Application Question 21: What insight into the interviewee is revealed from his statement that he does not want to "brag" about the dysfunctional status of his family?

Examining the Components of the Interviewee's Self-Description

"Do you have a set list of questions that you ask during the conduct of your fraud-related interviews?"

"Yes, usually I have an outline to help me remember topics and questions."

—Question submitted by an anonymous class participant

Teaching Point: Now let us closely examine what the interviewee has shared and explore its application to the interview. The salient points the interviewee has presented are:

- His family was dysfunctional.
- Although having a dysfunctional family is a status which could be boasted on, he will elect not to do so.
- His parents "were" divorced when he was three.
- His mother was having medical problems.
- He was living with his father.
- He has an older brother and two older sisters.
- He was the baby of the family.
- He was nine years younger than his next youngest sibling (sister).
- He discovered as a young child that he had the "knack" for being able to talk himself out of situations.
- He got in trouble in school.
- He got in trouble with his grandparents.
- When he got into trouble he talked his way out of it.
- It was "kind of tough growing up."
- His father and grandfather were in the bakery business.
- His father and grandfather did not get along.
- He was in the middle between his father and grandfather.
- He came from a broken home.

Developing Amplification Questions Regarding the Interviewee

The interviewee has provided a wealth of information — on which to build a more positive interviewer-interviewee relationship and formulate questions which bring forth additional information. At this point in the interview, the interviewer should rely heavily on open questions — what? how? why? could or would? — to encourage the interviewee to talk and set a more conversational tone to the interview. Examples of questioning options that can serve to open the interviewee, revealing more and more, include:

- You said your family was as "dysfunctional as they come," please tell me about that.
- How did you feel about having a dysfunctional family?
- You said your parents were divorced when you were three, what was involved in that circumstance?
- You said your mother had medical problems, would you tell me about them?
- What was it like living with your father?
- Would you tell me about your bothers and your sisters?
- What was it like being the youngest in your family?
- How did you discover you had a knack for talking your way out of situations?
- You referred to getting in trouble at school or with your grandparents. Would you give me an example?
- You said it was "kind of tough growing up." What do you mean?
- In what aspect of the bakery business were your father and grandfather involved?
- You said your father and grandfather did not get along. What did you mean?
- You said you were sometimes in the middle between your father and your grandfather. Would you give me an example?

- You indicated you came from a "broken home," What were the consequences on your life, as you see them from that broken home?

Once the interviewee has responded to a question regarding a salient point, the interviewer can explore that dynamic with additional questions as needed. When moving on to another descriptive element, the interviewer should once again employ an open question and amplify (use additional questions placed at specific points in the narrative to elicit additional information) when appropriate. Keep in mind that it is not, in and of itself, necessary to apply questions to each and every presented interviewee self-component. However, as is usually the case, interviewers run out of questions before interviewees run out of answers. Don't let that be the case with you. The prevailing purpose of the opening is to learn more and more about the interviewee.

With regard to relating to the interviewee and making the person to person connection, the interviewee has provided an excellent list of options. Most of us:

- have a family that is less than perfect;
- have gotten in "trouble" in school or at home;
- have or brothers and sisters, younger or older;
- have our own story with regard to it being "tough growing up";
- have at one time or another to talk our way out of trouble.

By listening closely and giving thought to what the interviewee is really saying, an interviewer would be hard pressed not to find some relating component of themselves which they can lay on the table, giving the impression that we are, after all, simply two people talking.

Return to the interviewee's response to Interviewing Inquiry 1

Exercise 1: Write down the salient points of the interviewee's self-description.

Exercise 2: Write an open question for each identified interviewee self-descriptive element.

Exercise 3: Based on what the interviewee has shared about himself, identify and write down five responses that you could have employed if you had been the interviewer.

Summary

In the fraud-related intervie w, no component is more important than the very beginning. A heavy sigh or a furrowed brow on the part of the interviewer speaks volumes to the interviewee who is reading the interviewer. The interviewer should strive to minimize the formality of the communication event and cause the interviewee to open up and reveal something of a personal nature. The idea that you are just people talking is paramount. Every component that the interviewee shares provides an opportunity for the interviewer to know more about the interviewee presents a possibility for relating to the interviewee and can, under the most ideal of circumstances, provide a direct link to the causality of the fraud and to an admission of the act committed. Interview Inquiries 1–3 provide the prelude to the interviewing symphony. This segment of the interview, wherein the interviewer endeavors to learn something about the interviewee, does not have to take an inordinate amount of time. This segment nevertheless comprises an important part of the overall process.

Chapter Take Away: The first few moments of the fraud-related interview are critical. The interviewee will quickly form an assessment of the interviewer. With regard to a productive interview outcome, the more positive the interviewer's initial impression, the better.

Interviewing Skill Enhancement Activity: Have someone who is a knowledgeable interviewer observe you conducting an interview. Ask that person to honestly provide an assessment of your interviewing communication skills, placing an emphasis on the first three minutes of your interaction with the interviewee. Take constructive criticism to heart and develop a plan to strengthen that communication component. All who strive to become better interviewers have to be open to the idea that there is certainly room for improvement and actively seek suggestions and recommendations to make it happen.

Examination: Chapter 1

The three steps to the opening segment of the fraud-related interview are:

1. _____

2. _____

3. _____

Once the opening question is asked, the interviewer should:

4. _____

5. _____

The goal of the opening is to:

6. _____

Once the interviewee has shared something of himself, the interviewer should:

7. _____

Summarize the steps of the opening of the fraud-related interview in three sentences.

8. _____

9. _____

10. _____

Chapter 2

Pressure/Motive: Company A

Inquiries 4 to 6

Application Question 1: Have you ever been placed in a situation wherein it was possible for you to convert money or other material to your own use? If so, what were those circumstances?

Application Question 2: Even for just a fleeting moment, did you ever think about doing that very thing?

Application Question 3: Could a circumstance—any circumstance—ever arise that would result in you converting money or other material belonging to others to yourself?

Application Question 4: If your children were starving, would you steal?

Interviewing Inquiry 4

Interviewer: Let's start with Company A.

Subject: Okay.

Interviewing Inquiry 5

Interviewer: Tell me what happened with regard to Company A.

Subject: Okay. I was employed as a controller for Company A. Basically, I was hired as controller there. In a company that was basically a part of a larger company. It was kind of a division. And they made units there that actually went into a bigger part of this company's business they were into. And which direction you want me to go into?

Interviewing Inquiry 6

Interviewer: From the very beginning of your criminal activity to the end as far as that particular company is concerned.

Subject: Okay. The way it basically got started was I had started an extramarital affair. And I was in the process of moving out of the home and moving to another city. And from that point on, during my work there we were in a growing time for the company. We were real busy and then as it did happen I got short on funds. Because here I was living two lives. And the opportunity came and presented itself for me to commit the fraud that I committed. I basically started and I wrote a check to myself. I had check-signing responsibilities with one of the other officers there at the company. And with the human resources director too. And as long as there were two signatures the checks would go through. I wrote one check to myself, deposited it into my bank there in town. Literally went through funds very, very rapidly. Through materiality, blowing money, blowing funds. And that perpetrated me doing another check. I wrote two checks to myself out of that company. Signed them and deposited them directly into my bank account.

Connecting the Interviewee's Life Circumstance(s) to the Possibility of Fraud

Teaching Point: Dr. Donald Cressey developed the classically known Fraud Triangle Model. Just as a fire has three elements which must be present for a fire to occur—heat, oxygen, and fuel—Dr. Cressey asserted for fraud to occur there were similarly three contributing factors. At the baseline of the triangle on the left is the *Pressure/Motive* factor.

Adverse financial circumstances arise in the lives of nearly everyone, but for some, a circumstance develops that, when combined with the presence of the two other elements—opportunity and rationalization (addressed in subsequent chapters)—results in the commission of fraud. Additionally, a circumstance that would have no effect at all on one individual committing fraud could prove to be very compelling to another. Again, this human characteristic that no one size pressure/motive fits all underscores the importance of learning as much as possible about the interviewee and seeking out those interviewee self-descriptive components for application emphasized in Chapter 1.

Pressure is defined as, "the emotional experience of feeling compelled to respond to someone's wishes or to external forces" (*Penguin Dictionary of Psychology*, 3rd ed.). Motive is defined as, "a state of arousal that impels an organism to action" (*Penguin Diction of Psychology*, 3rd ed.). In our examination of these two terms as they apply to the fraud-related interview, the significant words and phrases are:

- Emotional experience
- Feeling compelled to respond
- Someone's wishes or external forces,
- A state of arousal
- Impels
- Action

A Life Out of Control

Pressure/motive results in a loss of control in the life of the person committing fraud. The mindset for this type of person is either someone, some external force, or both, has created a circumstance resulting in a negative, emotional state for him or her. He or she now feels compelled to respond to action. The action in this case is fraudulent undertakings. The individual is attempting to reestablish equilibrium in his life *as he defines it.* The circumstances of the individual's life do not have to line up with the interviewer's evaluation of what defines a life out of control. The fraudulent actions taken on the part of the person attempting to return to normalcy do not have to reach the level of justification as perceived by the interviewer. The only world that matters, in which there are perceived pressures and actions taken to eliminate those pressures, is the interviewee's. The interviewer endeavors to *utilize* the pressure/motive cognitions of the interviewee. Taking the time and effort to *judge* the validity of the interviewee's pressure/motive cognitions contributes nothing productive to the outcome of the interview. Some examples of pressure/motive include, but are in no way limited to:

- Getting the kids through college
- Getting an aged parent through a medical crisis
- Keeping up with their associates
- A setback in the overall economy
- Salary or bonuses linked to performance or sales
- Salary or bonuses linked to students' end-of-grade exams

Application Question 5: In the interviewee's response in Inquiry 6, what was his pressure/motive?

Application Question 6: What were the consequences of his pressure/motive?

Teaching Point: The interviewee has related that he "started an extramarital affair"; he was "living two lives" and he "got short on funds."

Exercise 1: Compare the phrases "living two lives" and "that is a quick version of who I am" found in Inquiry 1 to Inquiry 3 located in Chapter 1. Together these phrases provide greater insight into the interviewee. The consummate interviewer must understand the interviewee has multiple versions involving "self" and must develop an understanding attitude. Honestly reflect on your own ability to accept nonjudgmentally the various versions of pressure/motive presented by those who sit across from you.

For the interviewee, life was out of control. In this case, the lack of funds defined the external force to which he had to respond. He required enough money to live two different lives. If, at this point, you are thinking, "That does not justify fraud," then you still have not grasped the point—what you think, your worldview is not the issue here. The only mindset having any relevance here is the mindset of the interviewee. Endeavor to focus externally on the interviewee and not filter what has happened or is currently going on in your own value system. Let us state this bluntly, succinctly and with your best interest at heart: No one hired (or will hire) you as an interviewer to project your worldview onto others. They hired (or will hire you) you to get to the truth. The truth is this person did what he did because he thought what he thought. The interviewer's calling is to understand the other's worldview and utilize that understanding to gain a successful resolution.

Read the following pressure/motive criteria described by the second person who committed fraud first presented in Chapter 1.

Subject: I have a wife who stays home with my two daughters. I wanted the best for them. I guess I was willing to do whatever it took to make sure they had whatever they wanted. If they wanted $200 worth of toys at Toys R Us, they didn't have to ask for it. I look back at the way that I was raised and my family … my grandfather had seven bakeries in the Midwest and I never really needed anything. And I wanted to be that kind of person.

Application Question 7: What was the articulated pressure/motive on the part of this interviewee?

Application Question 8: How did the interviewee connect the circumstances of his own childhood with how he wanted to be perceived by his wife and daughters?

Teaching Point: Our examination of this statement presents the following with regard to pressure/motive as articulated by the interviewee:

- His wife did not work outside of the home.

- He had two daughters.

- He wanted the best (as he defined it) for them.

- He was willing to do whatever it took to make sure they had whatever they wanted.

- When he was a child he had everything he needed.

- He wanted to be that kind of person.

At this point, the interviewer should note the interviewee has indicated that as a child he had all that he *needed*. His expressed desire was for his children to have everything that they *wanted*. His expressed pressure/motive was for them to have just that — all that they wanted without even having to ask for it. He was willing to do whatever it took (commit fraud) to make sure they had all of their (even unexpressed) wants met. For them not to have their wants met and for him not to be seen as that kind of person was, for him, a world out of control. The way to restore order in his world was to commit fraud, and thus obtain more money.

Always bear in mind the pressure/motive dynamic presented by the interviewee may or may not be the actual pressure/motive experienced by the interviewee which was the tipping point for the commission of the fraud. At the end of the day, it does not matter. The real pressure/motive may be too psychologically painful for the interviewee to present. If this is the case, don't try to make them do it. It may result in the interviewee closing down the interview itself. The goal is to discover a pressure/motive frame which is, for the interviewee, conducive to moving the interview forward. Always maintain an attitude that says, "If this pressure/motive rack is what the interviewee is willing to hang his or her hat on, it works for me."

Consequently, when conducting a fraud-related interview, keep in mind the saying "you can never step into the same river twice." Like a river, time and circumstance keep flowing.

The individual being interviewed, for whatever reason—operational or financial audit, responding to an anonymous tip or a more formal inquiry into a suspected fraud—may have been as honest as the day is long up unto a given point but then something happened in this person's life. Something he or she perceived as life-changing has occurred. Whatever happened resulted in this person's world being out of control. In his or her mind there is no other way to restore order than fraud. He or she could have been a valued, loyal, honest employee of the organization for decades but something happened in his or her life.

The interviewer may know this individual personally, as well as professionally, and had conducted numerous interviews with him or her as part of their job responsibilities. But the river moves on. Changing circumstances may produce a profound emotional experience on a person, compelling one to respond in an attempt to restore order to a world one perceives as out of control. That response may very well be fraud.

Exercise 2: A company has determined there is a $9.9 million shortage on the books. The woman to be interviewed (Jane) has served as the company's chief financial officer for the last six years. Because she is such a trusted employee, the company has never hired an outside auditor to check the books. Based on the information provided in Chapter 1 and here as well as your individual reflections on the application questions, develop an interview plan in writing for conducting the interview with Jane and write out the questions you would use.

Exercise 3: Recently, an elementary school teacher was sued when one of the checks from the Parent-Teacher Association (PTA) bounced. A review of the books revealed a $10,000 shortage. An interview is to be conducted with the former president of the association. She was president from October of one year until June of the following year. She is a mother of three children and had at least one child enrolled at the elementary school during the time she was president of the PTA. At this school, over 80% of the students are on a "meals for free" or a "reduced cost" status. Based on the information provided in Chapter 1 and here, as well as your individual reflections on the application questions, develop a written interview plan for conducting the interview and write out the questions you would use.

Exercise 4: Read the following letter.

From: Jane Doe
To: Tammy Fay
Date: November 7, 2____
Subject: Jump Rope for Health

Tammy Fay,
    I received your email from Mrs. _____ yesterday morning about "what happened to the money raised for the Acme Health Association (AHA) at _____ in June 2____". For the past three years I have raised money here at _____school for the AHA. My children have gone to/go to _____ school and I knew that Coach _____ had not done Jump Rope for Health in the past. When I saw that they were going to participate, I asked Coach _____ if she would like some help. She was very appreciative since she had little experience with the whole event. She began giving me the envelopes with checks and money. I had exchanged small bills for large to make room and to be counted. The event took place on a Friday and when it was over I took the rest of the envelopes and finished counting the money. Over the weekend, I finished the prize list and counted the money. The day I faxed the list to the AHA is the day I took the pre-stamped, addressed envelope to the post office on _____ Street. Without thinking I sealed the envelope with everything inside and put it in the mailbox. There was a little less than $800 in cash that I did not get a cashier's check for and the rest was per-

sonal checks written to AHA. In all, the total was $6,893. I talked to _____ and _____ (555-123-4567) at the AHA office several times. _____ said that the envelope could have had the old address and may have come back. I went to the post office to see if they had found the envelope, but it was not there. The last time we spoke, she said that when the envelope was put in the mail that it was no longer my responsibility. I went by the post office two times to see if they had ever found the envelope. The envelope is still missing and has not been returned or found. Please let me know what I need to do next. As I said before, I have been doing this for a few years and have never had any trouble.

Jane Doe

Based on the information provided in Chapter 1 and here as well as your individual reflections on the application questions, develop a written interview plan for conducting the interview and write out the questions you would utilize.

Application Question 9: Did you find yourself planning each interview based on the limited facts provided in the same way? What could be the advantages or disadvantages of doing so?

Application Question 10: After completing Exercises 2 and 3, did anything develop in your mind with regard to interviewing persons suspected of fraud? What about after you completed Exercise 4?

Application Question 11: Over time, what negative effect on the mindset of the interviewer do you think could develop after working fraud case after fraud case, audit after audit, and interview after interview?

Application Question 12: What steps do you think an interviewer must take to make sure the negative mindset does not prevail? Have you or do you think you could do just that?

Summary

Pressure/motive does not create a person who commits fraud. Pressure/motive activates the fraud gene within the individual, which lies dormant up to the tipping point. Circumstances *happen* in the life of an individual. Whatever or whoever it may be results in a perceived loss of control in this person's world. In an attempt to restore order, the individual sees fraud as the most viable option and responds accordingly. During the conduct of a fraud-related interview, the one who committed the fraud may or may not be sitting directly across from you. Engage each interviewee in a conversational manner and listen closely. The more the interviewee talks, the more you learn. The more you learn the more reliable your diagnosis and astute your interviewing options for effectively moving the interview, and ultimately the inquiry, forward to a successful resolution.

Chapter Take Away: Pressure/motive can serve to release a dynamic within an individual that has heretofore remained dormant. Sometimes the dynamic released leads to fraud. The fraud-related interview endeavors to gain insight into the interviewee in order to determine if there exists a pressure/motive component in that individual's life which is of such potency as to initiate fraudulent activity.

Interviewing Skill Enhancement Activity: Find an opportunity to engage someone you do not know in conversation. Listen for one descriptive event — positive or negative — going on in his or her life. A descriptive event could include a child starting college, changing or losing a job, selling a house, and so on. In your communication, focus on the descriptive event. Strive to have the individual articulate how the event has impacted his or her life. An effective interviewer must be able to steer the interviewee into specific personal elements and the resulting emotive reactions.

Examination: Chapter 2

The three elements of Dr. Cressey's Fraud Triangle are:

1. _____

2. _____

3. _____

Define Pressure:

4. _____

Define Motive:

5. _____

Define pressure/motive:

6. _____

The fraudulent individual is attempting to:

7. _____

List three examples of pressure/motive:

8. _____

9. _____

10. _____

Chapter 3

Opportunity: Company A

Inquiries 6 to 10

Application Question 1: How do you conceptualize "opportunity"?

Application Question 2: Is opportunity something that someone causes to happen or something that happens to someone?

Application Question 3: Are opportunities intrinsically always good?

Interviewing Inquiry 6

Interviewer: [Tell me about your actions] from the very beginning of your criminal activity to the end as far as that particular company is concerned.

Subject: Okay. The way it basically got started was I had started an extramarital affair. And I was in the process of moving out of the home and moving to another city. And from that point on, during my work there we were in a growing time for the company. We were real busy and then as it did happen I got short on funds. Because here I was living two lives. And the opportunity came and presented itself for me to commit the fraud that I committed. I basically started and I wrote a check to myself. I had check-signing responsibilities with one of the other officers there at the company. And with the human resources director too. And as long as there were two signatures the checks would go through. I wrote one check to myself, deposited it into my bank there in town. Literally went through funds very, very rapidly. Through materiality, blowing money, blowing funds. And that perpetrated me doing another

27

check. I wrote two checks to myself out of that company. Signed them and deposited them directly into my bank account.

Opportunity Knocks

Teaching Point: Dr. Donald Cressey's second element in the fraud triangle is *opportunity*. According to Cressey's theory, pressure/motive combines with opportunity for two-thirds of the combustible mixture. *Opportunity* is defined as "a situation or condition favorable for attainment of a goal" (Dictionary.com).

In the narrative from the person who committed fraud, the operative phrase is, "And the opportunity came … presented itself for me to commit the fraud that I committed." Let us examine the definition of opportunity and the words of the fraudster in light of the definition.

First is the attainment of a goal. The goal of this person is to restore order to his world. We have already seen perception of a loss of control which included an extramarital affair, leading two different lives and being short of funds.

Second is a favorable situation or condition. The favorable situation or condition that would allow the restoration of order was the ability to write a check to himself and deposit it in the bank. He did so once and then he did it once again. There are several revelations from the interviewee here serving to provide information to the attentive interviewer. Note the interviewee stated, "the opportunity came … presented itself for me to commit the fraud. " The interviewee constructs the phrase in such a way that it would seem that the "opportunity" is a sentient being. The opportunity "presented itself." The doer of the action is the opportunity.

Application Question 4: Why do you think the interviewee would present the concept of opportunity using the phrasing he did?

Application Question 5: What interviewing options for the interviewer are placed on the table as a result of the interviewee's opportunity-focused revelation?

The reality is that the opportunity never came. It did not have to. The opportunity never presented itself. It was not necessary. The opportunity was there *all along.* At any point, due to his position, the individual could have written a check to himself and deposited it in the bank. The real dynamic that changed was the loss of control in his life—the pressure motive. Only then did he see what had been there all along as an opportunity. His perception changed to one of a vulnerable, occupational circumstance which opened the door for the commission of fraud.

The importance of having the interviewee articulate organizational or operational business practices, processes, quality level standards, security controls, specific events, relationships, job-specific authorities, and so on cannot be overstated. Even if the interviewer knows all of these elements chapter and verse, the interviewee's articulation is what is important. The interview should be conducted as if this were the interviewer's first day on the job requiring detailed explanations about everything. The interviewer's knowledge, skill and ability should in no way serve to truncate the interview process. The interviewer and interviewee are not communicating to exchange policy and procedure verbiage as to how operations are supposed to work. They are communicating in order for the interviewer to learn how operations *really* work (or do not work) and to learn more about the interviewee. Notice the interviewee's usage of the pronoun "me" within his statement "the opportunity *presented itself for me."* The pronoun "me" is the recipient of the action of the verb. The interviewer should note and factor into the compliance-gaining phase of the interview the interviewee (in his assertion) did not go looking for an opportunity. The opportunity presented itself to him.

Interviewing Inquiry 7

Interviewer: So, let me make sure I understand this. The extra-marital affair began. You were living two different lives; both of them were financially costly. So you decided to sign a check to yourself. And how much was that first check for?

Secondary Questions

Teaching Point: Consider the use of this form of a secondary question throughout the conduct of the fraud-related interview. By periodically summarizing the information provided, the interviewer endeavors to keep the interviewee on track, moving forward and committed to what they have asserted up to that point. Additionally, the phrase, "So, let me make sure I understand this," is designed to convey to the interviewee the idea the interviewer is sincerely endeavoring to understand. The need to be understood is a powerful motivator. The three elements of the fraud triangle, linked with the perception on the part of the interviewee that he or she is understood, make a powerful amalgamation leading to the successful conclusion of the interview.

Subject: The first check was around $48,000 and some change.

Interviewing Inquiry 8

Interviewer: And you deposited it into your own account?

Subject: Yes sir.

Interviewing Inquiry 9

Interviewer: But if they required two signatures, how did you pull that off?

Subject: Well I forged one of the gentleman's signatures onto the check.

Interviewing Inquiry 10

Interviewer: I am not an accountant so you have got to help me with this.

Subject: Okay.

The Benefits of Suspending Ego

Teaching Point: Again, the interviewer must be able to suspend ego. By asking for help in understanding, the interviewer is endeavoring to facilitate a more positive interviewer-interviewee relationship by engaging the interviewee in a cooperative undertaking. When the interviewee is telling you about "things," he or she is telling you about themselves. The more the interviewee Is willing to "help" you understand, the better the prospects are for a successful interviewing outcome. The goal is to have the interviewee talk more about less, and all the while, the interviewer is listening and observing attentively.

Read the following opportunity-related criteria described by the second subject first presented in Chapter 1.

Subject: Everything was going well at home. I don't know what happened. I can't explain it. One day I saw an opportunity and I took advantage of it. And that opportunity was when I started one of my jobs as controller to do the salary payroll. I didn't do the hourly payroll. I had somebody that did the hourly payroll. I did the salary payroll. I believe the reason for that is they did not want other people seeing what the managers and the upper management made. So I did the payroll for about ten to twelve people on a bi-weekly, every other week basis.

It was my job to run the checks, to put the payroll and at the end of the month, who do you think reconciled the bank statement? And I think that is pretty common. Every month end I got the bank statement in, nobody else opened it. I opened it, reconciled the bank statement. So I, being the quick thinker that I am—and I guess I look at that as an asset or a liability—I saw an opportunity to take advantage of. Probably three months after I started, I decided to try it out. What I did the first time was I doubled my payroll. Okay, and I had an easy answer for that if I got caught right away. I would say, "It was just a mistake and I am going to fix it on the next payroll." So that was my excuse and that was my reasoning how I did this—how I committed this fraud the first time. I had just started three months prior so I wasn't due for a raise. I think I felt—putting myself back in those shoes—I wanted to give my kids and my family everything they needed material-wise. I wasn't thinking from a mental standpoint, from a physical being standpoint. I wanted to give them everything they needed, toys, stuffed animals, anything they wanted. I wasn't looking at the physical self of being with your children.

Teaching Point: Now let's look at the narrative once again with some key components highlighted and pose some questions. "Everything was going well at home. I don't know what happened. I can't explain it. One day *I saw an opportunity and I took advantage of it*. And that opportunity was, when I started one of my jobs as controller was to do the salary payroll. I didn't do the hourly payroll. I had somebody that did the hourly payroll. And I did the salary payroll. And I believe the reason for that is they did not want other people seeing what the managers and the upper management made. So I did the payroll for about ten to twelve people on a biweekly, every other week basis. It was my job to run the checks, to put the payroll and at the end of the month, who do you think reconciled the bank statement? And I think that is pretty common. Every month end I got the bank statement in, nobody else opened it. I opened it, reconciled the bank statement. *So I, being the quick thinker that I am—and I guess I look at that as an asset or a liability—I saw an opportunity to take advantage of.* Probably three months after I started *I decided* to try it out. What I did the first time was I doubled my payroll. Okay, and I had an easy answer for that if I got caught right away. I would say, "It was just a mistake and I am going to fix it on the next payroll." So that was my excuse and that was my reasoning how I did this—how I committed this fraud the first time. I had just started three months prior so I wasn't due for a raise. I think I felt—putting myself back in those *shoes—I wanted to give my kids and my family everything they needed material-wise. I wasn't thinking from a mental standpoint, from a physical being standpoint. I wanted to give them everything they needed, toys, stuffed animals, anything they wanted. I wasn't looking at the physical self of being with your children.*

Application Question 6: How would you contrast the stance of subject 2 with regard to opportunity with that of subject 1?

Application Question 7: Subject 1 indicated the "opportunity presented itself to me." Subject 2 said "I decided to try it out." From an interviewer's perspective, what is the difference?

Application Question 8: For subject 2, what are the articulated pressure/motive components in his narrative?

Application Question 9: What questions would you ask to gain an understanding of the phrase "I wasn't thinking from a mental standpoint"?

Application Question 10: How would you determine the difference in the interviewee's mind between a "mental standpoint" and a "physical being standpoint"?

Application Question 11: As an interviewer, why would you even concern yourself with understanding the interviewee's definitions of "mental standpoint" and "physical being standpoint"?

> **Teaching Point:** In his narrative, subject 2 places himself more in the driver's seat of the situation than subject 1. He uses phrases such as:
>
> - I saw
> - I took
> - I decided
> - I had an easy answer
> - I would say

Subject 1 passively had the opportunity present itself to him. Subject 2 actively sought the opportunity. Both end up at the same destination—committing fraud. Neither is less culpable than the other, but to the interviewer, how the individual positions himself to opportunity is important. It provides insight into the mental processes of the interviewee allowing the interviewer to understand and embrace the interviewee's position and begin to set the course for transitioning the interview into the compliance-gaining phase. But notice both subjects use the term "opportunity." Just as a hungry traveler will begin to look for road signs advertising eating establishments to satiate hunger, pressure/motive activates the individual to look for an opportunity to restore order in his or her life. To the traveler who is not hungry, signs advertising restaurants do not even register on the conscious mind. Likewise, the individual whose life (as they define it) is in a state of balance "drives" right past business practice situations that would lend themselves to the commission of fraud. Only when the pressure/motive hunger appears does the individual begin to look for signs of opportunity.

Philosophical questions as to whether an individual is a situational fraudster or a predatory one are certainly interesting and will be

addressed in Chapter 8. But to the interviewer in the room conducting the interview, the only reality that matters is the interviewee's. The true magnetic north in fraud-related interviewing is the
idea that *situations produce reactions.* People reveal that which is
within themselves as a result of their reactions to the situations.
For the interviewer, how the interviewee presents a response is the
only reality. The interviewer will utilize the interviewee's presentation to carry the interview forward.

Exercise 1: Read the following.

*A 42-year-old soccer mom has been arrested for embezzling
$72,000 from the school soccer club for which she was serving as
treasurer. The preliminary investigation has revealed she wrote
checks to her teenage son and to her landlord.*

You are responsible for planning and conducting an interview with
this woman.

Interview Preparation Question 1

In developing an interviewing plan, how will you factor in the
possibilities regarding pressure/motive into the conduct of the interview?

Interview Preparation Question 2

In developing an interviewing plan, how will you factor in the
concept of "opportunity" into the conduct of the interview?

Interview Preparation Question 3

In developing an interviewing plan, how will you utilize the implication that she wrote checks to her teenage son?

Interview Preparation Question 4

In developing an interviewing plan, how will you utilize the implication that she wrote checks to her landlord?

Summary

It has often been said that success happens when preparation and opportunity come together. In a similar manner, two-thirds of the fraud triangle is thus firmly in place when pressure/motive crosses paths with opportunity.

Chapter Take Away: Business operations are replete with opportunities for fraud. A business operation is performed by a person. Fraud becomes a distinct possibility when the person begins to perceive a business operation as an opportunity.

Interviewing Skill Enhancement Activity: In an informal, non-business-related setting, take the occasion to ask the question, "If someone were to divert resources from your organization (business, charity, club, team), what would be a way they could do it?" Watch and listen to the individual closely as they contemplate and respond. Afterward, ask them, "What would be another way?" Again, watch and listen. Now ask yourself, "What did I see and hear?" A consummate interviewer must be able to guide the interviewee beyond the borders of the cognitive comfort zone.

Examination: Chapter 3

Opportunity is defined as:

1. _____

By periodically summarizing the information provided, the interviewer endeavors to:

2. _____

3. _____

4. _____

The use of the phrase, "So let me make sure that I understand this" is designed to:

5. _____

When discerning opportunity, and interviewer must be able to:

6. _____

When an interviewee is telling about (7) _____

he/she is also telling you about (8) _____.

People reveal what is (9) _____

as a result of their (10) _____.

Chapter 4

Rationalization: Company A

Inquiries 11 to 41

Application Question 1: Have you ever been in a situation wherein you did something you normally would not do?

Application Question 2: Was it something which violated your own sense of right and wrong?

Application Question 3: How did you reconcile your actions in your own mind?

Interviewing Inquiry 11

Interviewer: In your mind, once you forged the signature, did you not have some idea that sooner or later this would come apart? And I want to ask, knowing what you know from your business experience, why would you deposit it in your own account?

Subject: People want to say that there was a lot of thought that went into it. There really wasn't. Now, I think a lot of it had to do with being diagnosed as manic depressive. I was basically in a very, very high state. And really got to the point where I thought things. I thought I had thought things through. From the standpoint of all the check reconciliation I did in-house. There wasn't some secondary person that did the check reconciliation. And so I, you know, the first check went through. I reconciled it. Nothing was ever said. It went all the way through check reconciliation. All the way into a drawer right beside my desk. And the balance sheet was done. The income statement done. It went on. So I guess from the standpoint of what I thought, I was just … everything was running so fast in my life, I really wasn't thinking about the consequences.

Rationalization

Teaching Point: In the foregoing response, the third component of the fraud triangle—rationalization—has now been placed on the table. Rationalization is be defined as "the process through which things that are confusing and obscure and irrational (or, better perhaps, non-rational) are made clear, concise and rational. The process serves as a defense mechanism to conceal the true motivations of one's actions, thoughts or feelings" (*Penguin Dictionary of Psychology,* 3rd ed.). With the sentence, "Now, I think a lot of it had to do with being diagnosed as manic depressive," the interviewee has, only four minutes into the interview, presented all three of the elements of the fraud triangle.

Within the conduct of the interview, gaining insight into the interviewee can provide the means to identify his or her rationalization for the act. Once rationalization has been identified, the interviewer will then endeavor to embrace the rationalization in a nonjudgmental style using the rationalization as a means to gain compliance. In comparing the fraud triangle to the fire triangle, think in terms of these frames:

- Pressure/motive is the heat. Someone or something has turned up the thermostat in this individual's life.
- Opportunity is the fuel. It is there providing the means for fraud—something to "burn."
- Rationalization is the oxygen. It enables the fraud/combustion to happen. Heat and fuel are not enough to start a fire. Similarly, pressure/motive and opportunity are not enough to generate fraud. But to heat and fuel add an appropriate amount of oxygen and you have a fire. To the pressure/motive and opportunity add an appropriate amount of rationalization and you have a fraud.

It cannot be overstated—within the conduct of the interview, learning as much as you can about the interviewee and his or her circumstances is critical to the successful outcome of the interview and the overall inquiry.

Exercise 1: Let's return to the situation we examined in Chapter 3.

A 42-year-old soccer mom has been arrested for embezzling $72,000 from the school soccer club for which she was serving as treasurer. The preliminary investigation has revealed she wrote checks to her teenage son and to her landlord.

You are responsible for planning and conducting an interview with this woman.

Interview Preparation Question 1: In developing an interviewing plan, how will you factor the concept of rationalization into the conduct of the interview?

Interview Preparation Question 2: What will be your alternate plan with regard to rationalization?

Interviewing Inquiry 12

Subject: I did in my head know that if the right checks and balances were put in place or if someone did an audit or something then I would probably get caught. Now getting caught was not a fear of mine at that time. Obviously, because I did it a second time.

Interviewing Inquiry 13

Interviewer: Tell me about the second time.

Subject: The second time I did it I did the same thing. I wrote myself another check, signed the signatures, deposited it the account. Now the second check is what got caught.

Interviewing Inquiry 14

Interviewer: How much was it for?

Subject: Another $50,000.

Interviewing Inquiry 15

Interviewer: Okay. Tell me about the second check.

Subject: Okay. The second check. After I deposited it in my bank account again. And it went through the bank and it came back with the checks from the bank to get reconciled. I was extremely busy at work. We were doing a lot of things. Well literally the young lady— and she was a very, very close friend of mine. So this really affected her having to do this. She opened the checks and decided to reconcile them for me to put them into the system. Well she was a very good employee. She saw that. It flew a red flag so she took it into the manager of the company. And that's how I got caught.

Interviewing Inquiry 16

Interviewer: Okay. So she was doing you a favor?

Subject: Yes sir.

Interviewing Inquiry 17

Interviewer: So it was her doing you a favor that began to cause this house of cards as it were to ...

Subject: ... start to crumble.

Interviewing Inquiry 18

Interviewer: Take me back to the day, and I understand you were dealing with some bipolar issues. Were you on any type of medication?

"For me within the interview it is not just being understood, but understanding as well when communicating with the interviewee."

— Anonymous class participant

Teaching Point: The need to be understood is vital to a person's (in this case the interviewee) well-being. Being understood means to the individual that he or she is in sync with the rest of the world.

Application Question 4: Have you ever heard someone assert, "No one understands me"? What do you think they were really saying?

Application Question 5: Has anyone ever said to you, "You just don't understand"?

Application Question 6: If the answer to the previous questions is "yes," what was your response?

Develop the Capacity to Always Understand

The consummate interviewer portrays an understanding attitude. People respond to those who understand them. It is not necessary for the interviewer to agree with the interviewee's rationalization, but rather to understand that it *is* the interviewee's rationalization.

Subject: Lithium. And I had gone off of it. So that was part of the problem.

Interviewing Inquiry 19

Interviewee: The day you wrote that check. I would like to know what was going on in your mind up to the point before you actually wrote that check.

Subject: From the standpoint of what was going on in my mind I just knew that the level of income I was making was not being able to support the things that I had going on in my life. Now, this is different from the situation when we get to Company B. This was totally different. This was greed. It was living a life that was very high above my needs ... my means. I literally do not ... when I think back and of course it was years ago. And I hope I am a little bit more mature today than I was then. But I can't understand people not seeing so much change in my life. I mean there was a new car purchased. There was all kinds of materiality things that people should have been able to see that was changing in my life.

Leaving a home with four children. Those kind of things you would have thought red flags would have been flying all over the place. But I have always been very successful at the jobs I've done so my success kind of overshadowed anything they thought might have been going on. So I don't know what was going on in my mind other than saying that it was just greed, need for funds. I had known that the first check did not get caught. It went through. I reconciled it. Nobody asked any questions. So I appropriated the second check.

Application Question 7: In the preceding response, what was the implied pressure/motive?

Application Question 8: What subtle indications of the shifting of responsibility from himself to external factors are presented?

Application Question 9: How could an interviewer use these shifts to gain compliance from the interviewee?

Application Question 10: What does the interviewee's reflective observation about himself reveal? "But I have always been very successful at the jobs I've done so my success kind of overshadowed anything they thought might have been going on."

Teaching Point: With regard to Application Question 10, always pay attention to the asides made by the interviewee. Often these can be some of the most viable windows into his or her state of mind. Asides are unguarded reflections or musings providing invaluable information to the attentive ear.

Interviewing Inquiry 20

Interviewer: Okay. You have written that first check. You have crossed that line.

Subject: Yes sir.

Interviewing Inquiry 21

Interviewer: In your interactions with the woman who was your friend and (was) doing you a favor before she discovered the check and dealing with the other people in the company, were you operating under a cloud of suspicion? Do they know, do they not know?

Subject: No

Interviewing Inquiry 22

Interviewer: So it never crossed your mind?

Subject: No. No. From my knowledge — of course after the arrest I had no contact with them. To my knowledge there wasn't any cloud of suspicion.

Interviewing Inquiry 23

Interviewer: You didn't feel like there was?

Subject: I didn't feel like there was.

Interviewing Inquiry 24

Interviewer: If somebody said anything, you didn't wonder in the back of your mind, "Do they know? Is this thing going to fall apart?"

Subject: My mind was running so fast at that time. I don't know how much you know about bipolarism (*sic*) but it really was running at such a speed that those thought processes really didn't run through my mind whether I would get caught or not. I was just busy doing what I was doing.

Interviewing Inquiry 25

Interviewer: Now the lessons learned for people — there were no scheduled audits completed on a regular basis? No outside audit that had a system of checks and balances within this company?

Subject: No. Now from what I know about the company — what I knew going in and working for them — they had a lot of good checks and balances at some of the other satellite plants. And the corporate office from my standpoint — from the accounting standpoint — just the debits and credits, they had, they were very sound. But they were in a growing mode and in that growing mode they were, there was so much money being spent and so much construction going on inside the plant and so much machinery and equipment being purchased that the cash flow through that plant was very high. That they didn't even, you know, to my knowledge they wouldn't even notice those size of checks. I mean we were paying out checks $170,000–$200,000 on a regular basis.

Interviewing Inquiry 26

Interviewer: So what is the lesson learned with regard to Company A—be sure and what?

Subject: Put the proper checks and balances in place. I think that both A and B—the other crime that we are going to talk about—could have been prevented with the proper checks and balances put into place. That no way should the person cutting the checks, printing the checks have signing authority. I have worked for other companies where the accounting department had nothing to do with signing the checks. They had that accountability in another location of the company. I think if that would have been done it would have prevented ... there was no way I could have done what I did if the proper checks and balances would have been put in place. Now, in my own life do I think I would have done something else? Probably at that point ... I don't know what I would have done. But I think they could have prevented—and I wish they could have. Now the outcome of this situation, I don't know if you want me to go into that yet?

Teaching Point: In the statement by the interviewee, the sentences "Now, in my own life do I think I would have done something else? Probably at that point ... I don't know what I would have done," are most instructive. Whenever you are preparing to conduct a fraud-related interview, always think in this manner: If this individual were going to commit fraud, what would be a way in which they could do it? Do not think, "What would be the way?" With the second question you will cease thinking once you identify a possible fraud mechanism. With the first question you will continue to think even after hitting on a viable fraud mechanism. When the pressure/motive is in play and the rationalization is in evidence, the individual *will find* an opportunity. Even if an audit reveals a fraud-susceptible business practice and rectifies the operation, the pressure/motive-rationalization duo will cause the individual to seek out another opportunity.

Compare the person committing fraud to a burglar. If a burglar is looking for a house to break into, he or she sees a house. The house has bars on the doors and windows, an alarm system symbol, a mean dog in the yard and a sign that says, "I have a gun and I love to shoot it." Having seen the house, the burglar is not going to say, "Well that house is pretty well protected so I will just stop being a burglar." No, he or she will find another more vulnerable house to break into. The same mindset is true with the person committing fraud. As the first subject indicated, even if a vulnerable business practice is eliminated, he or she will find another way. The subject never stops thinking and neither should the interviewer.

Interviewing Inquiry 27

Interviewer: I do. We're at that point (having been arrested) now.

Subject: Okay. After I was arrested … if … I say this so sincerely … if they would have punished me at that point the way I got punished for the second crime that I committed, I don't think you and I would be sitting here. The laws, because I was a first-time offender, the laws were very easy on me. My parents came in, bailed me out. They spent a lot of money. I had a good family and they took care of me at that point. And I basically got put on probation for that. I really do believe if I spent eight months in a jail like I did for the second crime, you and I wouldn't be sitting here. Because I absolutely learned so much of a lesson that I didn't want my life taken away from me the way it got done the second time.

Interviewing Inquiry 28

Interviewer: Let me go back to this—your friend has opened the bank statement and is reconciling the checks, she takes the check you have written, the second check to, who did you say, the CEO?

Subject: The president, he was actually general manager.

Interviewing Inquiry 29

Interviewer: Tell me what happened from that point to when you were arrested.

Subject: Basically, he brought me ... asked me in ... and he and I were real close. I mean, you have got to remember for six months I was his confidant, his controller, the person he went to for answers, financial answers to the company. And the check was lying there. And he has me, "Have you got an answer for this?" I told him, "I really haven't got an answer." And of course the human resources person was sitting there also. He basically gave me the opportunity ... said, "From the company's standpoint if the money is brought back within forty-eight hours, we're going to terminate you and this will be the end of it." Well I couldn't. I had already spent most of the money. And so from that point on he asked me to leave the building and I left the building. Two days later I was arrested.

No One Gets a Pass

Teaching Point: The interviewee's remarks, "and he and I were real close. I mean, you have got to remember for six months ... this guy ... I was his confidant, his controller, the person he went to for answers, financial answers to the company" are most telling for understanding fraud-related interviewing. No one is above suspicion. Confidants, controllers, friends, even relatives can, under the right pressure/motive-opportunity-rationalization environment, commit fraud. In conducting the fraud-related interview, the interviewer must find the balance of open-mindedness, allowing him or her to hold two separate thoughts; not assuming (judgment prior to inquiry) the interviewee *is* guilty yet open to the possibility the interviewee *could be* a guilty.

Interviewing Inquiry 30

Interviewer: Okay now. At the point when he had that check in front of him, was he aware of the second check? Or did he only know about the first check?

Subject: I told him about the first one. Right there. Right at that point I confessed up to everything because he was asking for that amount of money and I told him at that point, "That's not all the money." At that point I knew it was just a matter of minutes before they would find that there had been a second check.

Interviewing Inquiry 31

Interviewer: How much time passed between the first check and the second check?

Subject: About three months.

Interviewing Inquiry 32

Interviewer: Three months. Okay. Once you had done that ... and I appreciate the fact you weren't thinking that clearly ...

Teaching Point: It is worth saying again You as the interviewer need to be able to convey an attitude of understanding and an appreciation of the plight and circumstances of the interviewee.

Subject: Yes.

Interviewing Inquiry 33

Interviewer: But did you ever entertain the idea of paying it back or putting it back? If I can just get this resolved and make it right?

Subject: This is going to throw a loop into everything. During that one, no. During the first time I committed this crime I did not think … I did not think that I had a method of paying it back. And so I, no … I really didn't. I was really … and I really don't want to blame it on the bipolarism right now. I am at a stage in my life now that I don't know that I have ever been bipolar. I just know that I have been very greedy in my life. I have been … a lot of times in my life said, "Well, that's why I did this, that's why I did that." Well I don't take that line anymore in my life. I have got to be accountable for what I do. And so, at that point, I really didn't. I wasn't planning on putting it back into the company.

Interviewing Inquiry 34

Interviewer: So you got probation?

Subject: Yes sir.

Interviewing Inquiry 35

Interviewer: Now once you were arrested were you ever interviewed? Were you interviewed by a law enforcement officer or an investigator at that point?

Subject: No not for the first one. I really wasn't. Basically, because I had … when I was arrested I was … of course, I can't remember … there was some legal … My father hired an attorney and from that point … I mean … the attorney actually came to the police station and got me out of jail. And at that point I never was interviewed by anyone regarding how I did what until recently in my life.

Interviewing Inquiry 36

Interviewer: So the attorney stood between you and anybody who would want to talk with you?

Subject: Yes sir.

Interviewing Inquiry 37

Interviewer: Now we talked about the auditing aspects as far as the checks and balances, but you also said your behavior should have raised a red flag with somebody. What would you tell people who are in human resources? What advice would you have for them looking back?

Subject: Well, human resources people, you know probably know the people and the level of income they have and more about that individual than anyone—when they hire them. Or they should! And that gets into another whole story as far as backgrounds and that issue. They should know. And when they see someone making $50,000 a year as a salary and when they start seeing a lifestyle that exceeds their means and they ought to be able to have their hand on the pulse of what's going on within that company. I know if I hired a human resources person I would want them doing that. I would want them understanding what's going on. It is not personal but there would be ... there would be red flags. I mean I pull up in a brand-new $30,000 vehicle and they know my salary is $50,000, you know, I may not come point blank and ask but I would inquire you know. "Well how did ... ?" You know. You know in office talk "How could he afford that?" I would have been asking those kinds of questions.

Interviewing Inquiry 38

Interviewer: Knowing what you know now, if you could go back—if you were a human resources person—you are saying, "If I would have noticed this on the part of an employee or this would have been brought to my attention, I would have done something." What would you have done?"

Subject: I would ask questions or inquire. I know they are governed by laws in what they can and what they cannot ask and where they can stick their nose but there should have been some ... but if I ... if they see something like that there's nothing wrong with checking the company's policies on things. Checking to make sure the check reconciliation is being done properly. And going back through the accounting ranks making sure that what checks they did have in place were being done. And then once you have done that you've satisfied your curiosity.

Interviewing Inquiry 39

Interviewer: Looking at what it would be an individual would have access to, that if they were going to bring forth some type of fraud—these are their areas of responsibility, let's just make sure everything is squared away in their particular area?

Subject: Right.

Interviewing Inquiry 40

Interviewer: Okay. So you were arrested, your folks got you an attorney. They paid back the money?

Subject: They paid back most of the money at that point. Yeah, I am still paying ... I don't know exactly what the level that I am still paying. And there is an interesting twist to it. Because I deposited the money in the bank and they—the bank actually deposited it in my account without doing any of their checks and balances, or checking the signatures or anything. Who I am paying restitution to is actually the bank. I am paying restitution to the bank not Company A.

Interviewing Inquiry 41

Interviewer: I see. That is interesting.

Subject: Yeah it is interesting.

The Interview as a Part of the Flow

Teaching Point: Now that we have addressed pressure/motive, opportunity, and rationalization, let's put the *flow* of the fraud-related interview into perspective.

Read the following account of a fraud-related situation. You will be conducting the interview with a former manager that is suspected of stealing the money.

A 44-year-old man is suspected of embezzling nearly $346,000 from a fast food restaurant. Between September of one year and February of the next, 99 deposits totaling about $346,000 were missing from the restaurant. The individual was a manager at the restaurant during the time the money disappeared. He had worked at the restaurant for about five years and was fired February 15. He was located while working at another restaurant.

Planning for the Interview

An example of an interviewing plan would include:

- Gathering all of the supporting documentation related to the fraud. Becoming familiar with what you have and the reliability of the documentation.
- Conducting interviews with organization personnel and gaining an understanding of the operation, all the while keeping in mind the narrative says the individual was "a" manager at the restaurant not "the" manager. Keep in mind others may be involved collectively or on their own. Additionally, do not close your mind to the option that it is possible the individual may not be the one committing fraud.
- In the conduct of your interview with the individual, consider the following plan:
    1. Begin the interview as addressed in Chapter 1 — listening for windows into *pressure/motive and rationalization* (remember in example above the manager was fired);
    2. Allow the individual to explain the operation at the restaurant wherein the loss occurred to include as examples:
        i.   How deposits were made;

   ii.   Who made up the deposits;

   iii. Any system of checks, balances and verifications re-
         garding funds listening for indicators of *opportunity*;

3. Determine if there is anything else that the individual
   would like to add;

4. Ask the individual to assist you in clearing up some issues
   that have come to light;

5. Begin presenting the documentation and asking for explanations from the individual;

6. Evaluate the reactions of the individual;

7. Transition into the compliance gaining phase of the interview should the opportunity develop.

*"With regard to my fraud-related interviewing responsibilities the
elements I most want to achieve are structure, content, and closure."*

—Anonymous class participant

Perhaps the acronym FRAUD will serve to formalize the fraud-
related interview process. Think of it as follows:

F: Focus on the interviewee

R: Relate to the interviewee

A: Allow the interviewee to articulate

U: Utilize the conflicting information

D: Direct the interview toward gaining compliance

Exercise 2: Using the information found in the following narrative regarding missing money, develop an interview plan which
incorporates the information gained in Chapters 1–4 (opening,
pressure/motive, opportunity, rationalization) following the FRAUD
format:

*"Sunday morning started out smooth. I came in at about
7:45 to open. I found a note from my mother from the night before that said the she left the money that I need to open with on*

the top of the bags. I opened the safe about 10:10. Got the money and put it in the register. I closed and set the safe on day lock and began to open the store. About 11:45 Mary Smith (owner) came in and dropped off some stuff. I went about finishing up my work with dishes. When I got some customers (6–7), at approximately 13:50–13:80. The back door was not closed and during me making the sandwiches the safe was opened and most to all money was removed. I notice at about 13:85 that the safe had been opened and called the owner to see if she had taken the money. She said no and told me to call the police and ask the people up front if they had seen anyone in the back room. I never got a straight answer from them."

Exercise 3: Do the same with the following two narratives from the same individual. Include in your plan the sequencing of whom you would interview as well as the interviewing FRAUD format for each interviewee:

"I, Susan _____ closed Acme General at 8 pm on 4-27-_____. Patty _____ and myself finished checking out people at about 8:30. At this time, I started taking down the registers. As we arrived at the back door going into the stock room we both heard a noise. I put the registers into the office and closed and locked the office door. At this time we both looked around the store and under the clothes. We saw nothing. She finished cleaning and straightening the store, I was in the back office finishing the bank deposits and counting the drawers down. As I was finishing up Patty sat down at the break table to wait on me. When I finished I ask Patty if she had ever helped anyone hide the money. She said, "yes a long time ago." So I ask her to help carry the roll change, and she did. We then walked to the office to get my things when I remember to latch the back door and put the bar up. I then walked down to the breaker box and cut off the lights. We both then walked to the front of the store. We unlocked the door and we went out. I relocked the door and we went to the bank. Patty went her way and I went home."

4-30-20__

"I left my house at 730 am and went to pick up Jane _____. We went to McDonalds to get a cup of coffee but their computers were down. They said it would be about thirty minutes. So we went across the street to the Pantry. We both got a cup of coffee and I bought a pack of cigarettes. We went to Acme General where we saw Julie waiting for us Martie, Jane, and myself, then walked into the store. We went to the back room. Jane went to put her dress in the bathroom as I was going into the office. This is when I noticed the office was out of order. Drawers were open and papers were all messed up. I then told Jane to come here and we called for Martie to come to the door. Martie went into the office to check and make sure Robert's checkbook was there. We went out of the office and I noticed that the back door was unlocked. I told both Jane and Martie that that door had been locked. We then went to check on the money. Seeing that the rugs were messed up we didn't touch anything. We went to the front of the store to call Robert. He was already on his way to the store. When Robert arrived about 8:05 we told him what happened. He then looked it over himself and he called the police officer.

Susan _____

4-30-20__

Summary

Rationalization is the honey that makes any internal conflict "go down" a lot smoother in the individual contemplating fraud. If there is any bitter taste, honey-flavored rationalization will cover both the act and the aftertaste. Consequently, the fraud-related interviewer searches for that same honey and serves it back to the interviewee to make the act of admission "go down" just as smoothly.

Chapter Take Away: Rationalization is a fundamental component of the fraud triangle. In the commission of fraud, pressure/motive presents a need and opportunity provides a way. However, rationalization imparting the justification for the act completes the triangle and makes the behavior palatable to the individual.

Interviewing Skill Enhancement Activity: Videotape a Sunday morning discussion news show involving multiple participants. Watch the session several times noting any rationalizations that are provided by the various participants. Listening for rationalizations is a vital interviewing skill.

Examination: Chapter 4

Define rationalization

1. _____

Within the conduct of the interview, gaining insight into the interviewee can provide:

2. _____

Once rationalization identification has been made the interviewer should

3. _____ using the rationalization as

4. _____

Explain the role of the need to be understood in the human dynamic:

5. _____

6. _____

Whenever preparing to conduct a fraud-related interview, always think in this manner:

7. _____

8. No one is _____.

Relate rationalization to gaining compliance in three sentences.

9. _____

10. _____

11. _____

Chapter 5

Pressure/Motive: Company B

With regard to my interviewing responsibilities, the skill I most want to develop is the ability to gain an understanding of what to expect and look for in order to conduct an effective fraud-related interview to not miss important details, or signs.

—Anonymous class participant

Inquiries 42 to 55

Interviewing Inquiry 42

Interviewer: Tell me what happened from the point—probation, no prison time—to the present.

Subject: Okay. Of course there are certain skills that I have in my life and then of course I started looking for other work. And I was sending out resumes. And that's when I got introduced to Company B. Interviewed with the president of the company who had had years and years of experience in the industry but he again—it was a brand-new small—not a brand-new, an old company that was ready to take the next step and start growing. I went in, interviewed with him, second day he called me back for an interview and hired me. This is where I think a lot of people need more things too. And I know I put them in place in the business that I am in now is background checks. If they had done a background check on me prior to hiring they would have never put themselves in the situation where I perpetrated in Company B.

Interviewing Inquiry 43

Interviewer: So, in Company B you're going in the door as what?

Subject: As basically a resume that was doctored and interviewing and I went in as a controller.

Inviting the Fraudster into the Fold

Teaching Point: In a very real (though not technical) sense, the initial fraudulent activity began prior to employment with Company B. In this case, the deception was with the resume. In planning for the conduct of an interview, reviewing and verifying the veracity of the content of the interviewee's resume are appropriate steps to take. If the individual being interviewed has been deceptive on his or her resume or application, there is good reason to believe he or she will be deceptive in other aspects of their professional life.

Interviewing Inquiry 44

Interviewer: Tell me how you doctored your resume.

Subject: I just basically made up for the time of not including Company A in the resume. I just extended the time that I was with another company.

Interviewing Inquiry 45

Interviewer: At the time when you put together that resume and you were looking for employment, where are we as far as the bipolar issue?

Teaching Point: Note the use of the collective pronoun "we" by the interviewer. The use of "we" by the interviewer can serve to soften the conversation and make it a collective undertaking rather than an accusation.

Subject: Of course it was court-ordered that I had got back on the medication. And so I was on medication at that time. I don't know from the standpoint of what did it change. Why did I stop taking it? I usually do though start thinking, "Why do I need this?" And again, at the time that the crime was committed I had pulled myself off the medication. But that is no excuse. I don't want to use that as an excuse.

Interviewing Inquiry 46

Interviewer: I appreciate that. I am just saying, I am trying to understand at the point where you begin to fabricate your resume— to be deceptive on your resume.

Exercise 1: Explain the use of "I appreciate that" and "I am trying to understand." in Inquiry 46. Identify terminology an interviewer should try to avoid at this point in the interview dealing with the resume. Give three examples of how Inquiry 46 could have been made to minimize the possibility of a negative outcome.

Subject: Exactly. That's a good point. I had to have work. Trying to make some kind of income. I did not ... the level of income I had been able to make ... I didn't see me ever being able to make that kind of income if I had went and just basically told someone "This is my past, this is what I have done, are you going to give me a chance?" And so I fabricated it in order to be at a level of income that I thought I should be at.

Exercise 2: Explain what the interviewee reveals about himself when he remarks, "And so I fabricated it in order to be at a level of income that I thought I should be at."

Exercise 3: Explain the interviewee's use of the words "thought" and "should."

Exercise 4: Link both "thought" and "should" to the rationalization process.

Interviewing Inquiry 47

Interviewer: I understand. But (your) coming in the door was under a false pretense, as it were.

Subject: Yes.

Interviewing Inquiry 48

Interviewer: Did you go in the door with Company B with the idea, "I am going to do right while I am here"?

Subject: Absolutely. I gone through this in my life in the past thinking, "Okay, what I done in the past is the past and I am going to go in here and do the best job that I can do." And that was my total intention at the time. I had no intention of ever doing anything wrong in the company.

Application Question 1: The interviewee has revealed significant information in his use of an aside as he responds to Inquiry 48. Exactly what has the interviewee revealed to the attentive interviewer?

Interviewing Inquiry 49

Interviewer: Okay. Day one—Company B—false resume, here's your office (you now have the job under a false resume). Take me from there.

Subject: Okay. Basically the company was a small, family-owned company here in town. And that is a lot of the reason why they did not do a lot of background checks. But the gentleman that had come in—they hired a new president and the board of directors at that time—was ready for the company to take the next step and start growing. And I had a big part in that. We did. We took the company from, when I went into, the day I was employed the balance sheet-income statement was about 5.7 million a year was the revenue. When I left, it was thirty-eight to forty-two; was going to be in that range. We had taken a very small revenued (*sic*) company up to being a very big revenued company in just a short period of time that we were there.

Exercise 5: Read the interviewee's response to Inquiry 49 once again. Down the side of a sheet of paper, make a list of the pronouns used by the interviewee. Explain what the pronoun utilization by the interviewee discloses to the attentive interviewer.

Interviewing Inquiry 50

Interviewer: That was over six times.

Subject: Absolutely as far as revenue. Now the income did not go up six times.

Interviewing Inquiry 51

Interviewer: Tell me about the work schedule. You come in there; you are bound and determined to work hard. How many hours did you work with that company?

Subject: It was a lot of hours. We started early in the morning, left late at night for the first eight to ten months. We were really busy. Probably sixty-five to seventy hour work weeks, I think what it was. Growing, growing, actually throughout my tenure — while the president was still living — I mean I got a promotion from being controller to being VP. I was actually put on; basically made an officer of the company. And again, doing really well, the company is really growing. Really busy trying to put systems in. All the good stuff that was supposed to be going on.

Interviewing Inquiry 52

Interviewer: When you got promoted, did the president leave?

Subject: No, actually the president passed away.

Interviewing Inquiry 53

Interviewer: Did someone move up into his place?

Subject: That was a big part to where the problem comes in.

Interviewing Inquiry 54

Interviewer: Tell me about that.

Subject: They … I am going to throw some numbers around so that people can see the relationship and a little bit about why I felt the way that I did. The president was at 250,000 plus. That was his salary. At that time as a VP, I was making sixty-five. And at his death—well the company, due to all the things that I and the president—we had had several board meetings, we had been to various cities and states doing presentations. Well, they thought that they were going to give me the position. And you can imagine at that point I knew what he made and I knew what I made. I thought, "This is going to be a great opportunity for me." Well they bring me into a meeting with the board and they give me a $15,000 raise and tell me that I am going to run the company. And I get, not upset but I was upset. I thought a little bit, "The audacity." And this goes in a little bit—you have to know some of the background—the reason why the revenue had gone up quite a bit, I really thought was primarily the work that I and the quality control director had done at that plant. And what we had done; we had got them from being a mom and pop 'til we started doing government contracts. And so we started producing loads and loads of product for the government which took the revenue straight up. Now it wasn't the most profitable so you didn't see such an increase in income but you did see the revenue change and product flowing through there. Our price point on all the raw materials was going down because we were able to buy in quantity. And so the company had really got a whole lot better and I really thought I deserved, at that point, more income level than going from where he was—from sixty-five to eighty. Now that's what started permeating me having some ill will toward the company.

Exercise 6: Read the interviewee's response to Inquiry 54. Once more on a sheet of paper make a list of the pronouns used by the interviewee. Explain the changes in the pronoun utilization by the interviewee in response to Inquiry 54 in comparison to his pronoun usage in his response to Inquiry 49. Explain why the frequent usage of the third person pronoun "they" is important for the interviewer to note.

Interviewing Inquiry 55

Interviewer: I see.

Subject: And at that point it's totally different from the crime the first time. I [was] feeling like they owed me more money than they were paying me. And so there was opportunity and so I started myself again, cutting checks to myself. And not to the level that I did at Company A. These were just small checks and basically trying to get myself compensated to the level I thought I should be compensated at.

Exercise 7: Diagram the fraud triangle with the terminology utilized by the interviewee in his response to Inquiry 55 as it relates to pressure/motive.

It Is Not Always about Money

Teaching Point: The interviewee's response to Inquiry 55 is important to note. Pressure/motive does not have to be financial. Angst can serve readily as the pressure/motive element of the fraud triangle. Consequently, within the conduct of the interview, try to ascertain the interviewee's true feelings with regard to the organization's personnel. Most interviewee's are not going to see their position, organization, or supervisors as perfect. That is not the issue. What the interviewer is seeking is the individual with real angst with the organization, personnel, board, or the way they have been (or are being) treated.

Summary

Exercise 8: Summarize the lessons learned from the inquiries made and the responses given by the interviewee in Inquiries 42–55.

Chapter Take Away: Pressure/motive originates from many reasons having nothing to do with a financial need. However, the end results are the same — fraudulent behavior. An individual whose financial well-being is excellent can nevertheless perceive a wrong or other adverse action on the part of an organization which will work just as well to serve as the initiating dynamic.

Interviewing Skill Enhancement Activity: In your conversations with others — formal or informal — listen for their articulations of various, nonfinancially-related pressure/motives present in their lives. Note what they have to relate about those circumstances. Keep a list of those circumstances and review them periodically. An interviewer should be acutely aware of the various guises in which pressure/motive can manifest and not limit the factors that can contribute to an individual's possible involvement in financial fraud.

Examination: Chapter 5

Explain the difference (for the interviewee) between the pressure/motives for Company A and Company B:

1. _____

2. _____

Explain the consequences for each of the two pressure/motive circumstances:

3. _____

4. _____

How was the subject's employment interview similar to a fraud-related interview?

5. _____

6. _____

What was the interviewee's work schedule and productivity levels while at Company B prior to his fraudulent activities?

7. _____

8. _____

How did his perception of his organizational productivity contribute to his commission of fraud?

9. _____

10. _____

Chapter 6

Opportunity: Company B

Teaching Point: John James Ingalls (1833–1900), in his work titled *Opportunity*, describes the concept of *opportunity* as, "MASTER of human destinies am I." As you read and reflect on the interviewee's account of his fraudulent activities in Company B, keep in mind the role of opportunity as it continues to be a primary motivating element in his mind. With the words, "(A)nd there was opportunity." the interviewee initiates an undertaking, "and so I started myself again, cutting checks to myself," that destines him once more to commit fraud. In your preparation for the conduct of the fraud-related interview, do not underestimate (as many interviewers do) the role of opportunity. Its role within the interview is no less important than pressure/motive or rationalization. It takes all three elements for fraud to occur. In like manner, all three can greatly assist in determining the outcome of the interview itself.

Inquiries 56 to 65
Interviewing Inquiry 56

Interviewer: I see.

Subject: And at that point [the commission of fraud at Company B]—it's totally different from the crime the first time. I was feeling like they owed me more money than they were paying me. And so there was an opportunity and so I started myself again, cutting checks to myself. And not to the level that I did at Company A. These were just small checks and basically trying to get myself compensated to the level I thought I should be compensated at.

Exercise 1: Diagram the fraud triangle with the terminology utilized by the interviewee in his response to Inquiry 56 as it relates to opportunity. Explain the opportunity element as articulated by the interviewee.

Interviewing Inquiry 57

Interviewer: So in your mind, you were just making things right.

Subject: Yes, but that is a manic-depressive mind.

Exercise 2: Explain how the interviewee avoids the implications of guilt in the statement, "So in your mind, you were just making things right."

Interviewing Inquiry 58

Interviewer: I understand. I am just saying, your mind at that particular time—as you say—you got the promotion, but you didn't get the compensation you felt was suitable for somebody taking on that much responsibility.

Subject: Yes sir.

Exercise 3: Explain how the interviewer's summarization of the interviewee's mindset at the time of the commission of the fraud is important to an overall positive outcome of the interview.

Interviewing Inquiry 59

Interviewer: Did you ever say to somebody, "You know, I think I deserve more money"?

Subject: Yes sir.

Interviewing Inquiry 60

Interviewer: Tell me about that.

Teaching Point: Pay close attention to the pronoun usage in the interviewee's narrative regarding the circumstances of his promotion and the issue of compensation.

Subject: During that meeting when they gave me the raise we had a confrontation right there. The guy—no matter how strong the board of directors are, there is always a couple that are going to be leading the pack. And the two that were leading the pack at that point basically were argumentative with me. They said, "Well this guy had so many years of experience." I said, "Well I don't care—I mean, I know you guys are looking in thinking what this gentleman was doing but let me tell you the real story of how we have been going and how we have been doing and how we're getting there." And ... and so but it didn't work. They said, "If you are not satisfied with that, we'll go out and hire a president to come in and you can work for [him or her]."

Application Question 1: What does the interviewee's repeated use of the pronoun "they" indicate to you?

Application Question 2: How would you incorporate this linguistic dynamic into the conduct of the interview from this point forward?

Interviewing Inquiry 61

Interviewer: At this point you were placed in the dilemma wherein you could stay where you were at your current salary and work for somebody else or you could take the promotion at the salary that was nowhere near what you felt like you should be making?

Exercise 4: In Inquiry 61, the interviewer summarized the situation as articulated by the interviewee. Write a summary of the interviewee's narrative with regard to Company B in your own words. Read your summary out loud as if you were speaking to the interviewee. Honestly critique yourself as to how it sounds to you. Make any changes to your summary that would enhance its effectiveness. Read it out loud again. Repeat until you think you have it right.

Subject: Yes sir.

Interviewing Inquiry 62

Interviewer: During this same time, were there any of these expenditures as far as the material aspects that you were talking about; are you buying a lot of fancy stuff, buying new cars living the high life, or are you just working hard?

Pronouns and the
Information They Contain

Teaching Point: In the following response from the interviewee, pay particular attention to the repeated use of the pronoun "we." "We" indicates collective behavior or a collaborative undertaking.

Subject: No. I was basically working pretty hard at that point. What we had to do at the … the part that I was missing on my resume to be able to take the company where we were going — the first thing that I did, and that's what the board actually said, is probably one of my biggest strengths was putting the right people in the right place to actually make me look good and everybody else look good. So the first thing I did, I had to go out and get a marketing person. Because if we were going to continue to grow at the pace that we did — I had no marketing or sales background at that point. I had to have a marketing salesperson. So I went out and actually I put an ad in the paper and we finally found someone who was excellent and he is running the company today. That was totally qualified to do it. Literally — and this always shocks everyone — his salary was going to be $20,000 more a year than mine was. And I was hiring him to work for me because that was what he was going to demand. That's what his skill set demanded. And so we hired him on as marketing salesperson making more money than I was at that time.

Application Question 3: As the interviewer in a fraud-related interview, how would you adjust the conduct of your interview after having picked up on this repeated use of the pronoun "we"?

Application Question 4: What effect do you think hiring someone at $20,000 more than him would have on the interviewee's interaction with opportunity?

Application Question 5: If a revelation to this effect were to arise during the conduct of your interview, how would you apply this information?

Application Question 6: If another reader of this text were to respond to Question 5 with, "I would not incorporate this information into my interview," how would you respond to them?

Interviewing Inquiry 63

Interviewer: And the board of directors approved you hiring somebody at a salary that was $20,000 more than you and that person (with the higher salary) was answering to you?

Subject: Yes sir.

Interviewing Inquiry 64

Interviewer: They didn't say …

Subject: Oh they asked me, "Why? What is your rationale behind this?" I said, "I think the guy is worth this. This is his past salary range that he has been in. This is the company—the history that he has with other companies." I told them, "This is the right guy for the job." And it has proved out that I was right about that. He was extremely qualified to do the job.

Interviewing Inquiry 65

Interviewer: And I don't doubt it, but I just find it interesting they took your word when you said he deserved more money but they didn't take your word when you said you deserved more money.

Subject: Right.

Instigating Statements

Teaching Point: Inquiry 65 is an example of an instigating statement. Rather than asking a question, the interviewer has elected to provoke a response from the interview by making an assertion. In this circumstance, the interviewer has identified the angst generated within the interviewee by not receiving a salary he felt was commensurate with the responsibility of his new position. The interviewer has embraced the mindset of the interviewee and added to the angst by also seeing the inequity on the part of the board by bringing in a subordinate into the organization with a significantly higher salary than the president. The interviewee confirms that the interviewer has successfully connected with the interviewee with his one word response, "Right."

Application Question 7: How else could you have made the point in Inquiry 65?

Exercise 5: Review Inquiries 56–65 once again. On a sheet of paper, list all of the instances where the interviewee answered in the affirmative. Explain the advantage for the interviewer who is capable of maneuvering the interviewee into answering in the affirmative.

Exercise 6: Read the following.

A 41-year-old woman has been charged with taking $30,000. It has been reported that she made unauthorized credit card purchases and wrote company checks to herself to carry out the embezzlement.

You are responsible for conducting the interview. In the development of your interview plan, address the following:

- What documentation would you have on hand during the conduct of the interview?
- What could the documentation possibly inform you with regard to pressure/motive?

Exercise 7: Summarize the lessons learned from the inquiries and the responses in Inquiries 56–65.

Examination: Chapter 6

What is the difference, as articulated by the interviewee, between a manic-depressive mind and his own cognitions?

1. _____

2. _____

The interviewee stated in Inquiry 60, "We had a confrontation." Why is this statement important for the interviewer to note?

3. _____

4. _____

How could an interviewer use this information in the conduct of the interview?

5. _____

6. _____

Describe how the interviewer enhanced the interviewee's negative feelings in Inquiries 63–65.

7. _____

8. _____

9. _____

10. _____

Chapter 7

Rationalization: Company B

Inquiries 66 to 106

Interviewing Inquiry 66

Interviewer: Certainly, that [the board of directors approving a higher salary for a subordinate] had to produce a certain amount of angst in you.

Teaching Point: Inquiry 66 is another example of an instigating statement. Note the telling response it produced in the interviewee.

Subject: It did. It did. It created a lot of anxiety in me and about those times too, the funds that I started funneling to myself started about the time that the anxiety got pretty heavy.

Application Question 1: Think of a significant situation wherein you felt that you had been treated unfairly. What was your first response?

Application Question 2: Did it cross your mind to respond by doing something that would either get back at someone or serve, in your mind, to make things right?

Application Question 3: By reflecting on your own response in a given situation, can you better understand (but not necessarily agree with) how an individual may react to their own situation by committing fraud?

Exercise 1: Diagram the fraud triangle with the terminology utilized by the interviewee in his response to Inquiry 66 as it relates to rationalization. Explain the rationalization element as articulated by the interviewee.

Angst and Its Possible Role in the Commission of Fraud

Teaching Point: An employee arrested for stealing from her employer noted, "If she treated me better, with more respect, I probably wouldn't have done this," "I didn't steal from _____ because she treated me well. I only stole from people who didn't treat me with respect." As an interviewer, foremost in your mind should be "The more I know about this interviewee, his or her relationship with the organization, current life situations, and level of contentment, the greater my chances are for a successful interviewing outcome."

Interviewing Inquiry 67

Interviewer: Looking back, do you think the fact that, not only your inequity as far as your pay but the disparity between what someone that works for you was making and what you were making—do you see that as a precursor that began to cause you to do that?

Subject: Do I think ... you know I have answered that question a million times lying around at night. If I had brought him in at a lower rate—did that push me over—do I think I still would have if they had not done anything about adjusting my salary? Do I think I would have still tried to funnel funds to myself? And the answer to that is "Yes." Now the gentleman that I hired making more was a thorn in my flesh but I really at that time ... and not only did I hire him at a certain salary, but at the time too he had some personal medical bills that were associated with a child of his that I didn't ask for an approval [for payment]—but it was like somewhere between 17–20,000 and I cut a check and helped him so that we could get him on board. That was how important I knew this gentleman was going to be to the future success of the company.

Interviewing Inquiry 68

Interviewer: You labeled him as "a thorn in your flesh." Are you talking about the salary or him as an individual?

Teaching Point: In the fraud-related interview, it is important to pay attention to the terminology utilized by the interviewee and integrate those same terms and phraseologies into your vocabulary as you explore specific issues. If the interviewee references someone as a "thorn in my flesh" then you, as the interviewer, make the same reference when you probe for a more expansive explanation of the phrase and its meaning for the interviewee.

Subject: No. Him as an individual was wonderful. No. Nothing that this gentleman ever did or said or anything was negative toward me. He supported me. Even though I think he probably sat over thinking he was probably more qualified for my job than I was from the standpoint of having the whole gamut of responsibility. From the financial side, he had no knowledge, he was not an accountant. As so I think that's where he ... but he did his job well. We continued to grow the company. We had new accounts coming on board due to this gentleman. The thorn was not him it was that he was actually making more money than I was.

Interviewing Inquiry 69

Interviewer: Was he appreciative of the fact that you signed a check for 17,000?

Subject: Very. Extremely I think he was.

Interviewing Inquiry 70

Interviewer: You said the checks that you were starting to write now were smaller checks.

Subject: Right.

Attending to Every Word

Teaching Point: Again, listen, pick up on the terminology of the interviewee and reflect it back in your communication with him — in this case "smaller checks" — see the response to Interview Inquiry 56 in Chapter 6.

Interviewing Inquiry 71

Interviewer: But were there more of them?

Subject: Yes sir.

Interviewing Inquiry 72

Interviewer: Tell me about that.

Subject: Okay. The amount ... the total amount — and this gets into a very hard subject for me because the money ... and I am going to say this and then we'll go back to that if you don't mind. The money that I am literally paying them back is not literally the funds ... the checks that I wrote. I mean because ... now this gets into another situation where I was in a relationship. The money I am paying back is actually the expense stuff that was the credit card; traveling and all that stuff that they said were not approved. When I was arrested it was $34,000 and that is what I am still paying back to them. Now the $117,000 that over the nine months that I was writing myself checks ... not nine months ... May–December ... seven months. The money that I wrote ... that was in little, small, little bitty checks ... I mean 5,000 here, 7,000 there. That's how I did. I didn't write any $25,000 checks to myself or along those lines.

Interviewing Inquiry 73

Interviewer: Within Company B was there a system of checks and balances or could you just sign a check?

Subject: No. I could period. My signature was it. Which was crazy.

Interviewing Inquiry 74

Interviewer: Was there any type of audit review or checks and balances as you say?

Subject: The lady that did the work for me did the reconciliation. Now I do think that this lady ... she had been with the company about twelve to fifteen years. I can't remember the exact number. She had been with the company a long time. I do think that she suspicioned (*sic*) the checks that she was reconciling going in but she went on with it. She never did bring it to my attention, or to my knowledge [never] brought it to the company's attention.

Interviewing Inquiry 75

Interviewer: While all of this was going on did you have some indication that she had some suspicion?

Subject: A little bit.

Interviewing Inquiry 76

Interviewer: What specifically was going on that made you think she had a suspicion?

Subject: Because I knew how good she was. And I know how loyal she was to the company. I just felt ... I don't know what it was ... I can still feel it today that she felt an uneasiness about what she was doing.

Interviewing Inquiry 77

Interviewer: When you were communicating?

Subject: Yes sir. And when ... you know, when the reconciliation— she'd bring the reconciliation to me and all the checks and everything. Because I required all the accounts and the general ledger to be reconciled at month's end. And it was just a funny feeling I had. I thought that she had some, you know, knowledge of what was going on.

Interviewing Inquiry 78

Interviewer: Okay.

Subject: Now after the fact she really did, I think, from the standpoint of what I know.

Interviewing Inquiry 79

Interviewer: What caused this house of cards to come down?

Subject: I guess from the standpoint of ... there was an audit required. They came in and ... we were using a very low ... I guess ... low-powered accounting system. And there had become some issues; the balance sheet and the income statements and those kinds of things. So they actually came in and were trying to reconcile the accounts. And so the external auditors actually caught that I had actually done something. They started questioning some of the checks being written.

Interviewing Inquiry 80

Interviewer: You said there were some issues which came up that caused this audit to occur. This is not something that happened on a regular basis?

Subject: Yes sir?

Interviewing Inquiry 81

Interviewer: This is not something that happened on a regular basis as far as this audit, if I am understanding you correctly.

Subject: Well they were supposed ... they were doing ... every six months they were doing an internal audit. And actually one of them ... I had actually passed through the internal audit after ... after some stuff had been done.

Interviewing Inquiry 82

Interviewer: Okay. Let's talk about that.

Subject: Okay.

Interviewing Inquiry 83

Interviewer: You are already doing "some stuff," as you say, and you are passing through this audit. This is the time when the auditor is there with you within that division.

> **Teaching Point:** Note how the interviewer reflected the interviewee's phrase "some stuff" in Inquiry 83. Paying attention to the terms utilized by the interviewee and reflecting those same terms back into the dialogue serves to engender understanding and enhance the communication process.

Subject: Yes sir.

Interviewing Inquiry 84

Interviewer: Tell me about that time.

Subject: Oh it was a nerve-wracking period of time—for me it was. Because at that point it was like in June that they did the six-month audit. And there hadn't been a lot of funds taken at that point. It was just very, very little. And I was a nervous wreck, literally. But they came in, did all the checks and balances that a midterm audit was supposed to be doing. And then they never asked any questions. They … I don't know that they just didn't pull the right checks to check. Because they would go through and pick certain checks and then do and audit. Do a test, what they called them and never caught anything that was out of kilter at that time, even though there had been some crime already committed.

Exercise 2: Note the highlighted terms and phrases in this re-reading of the interviewee's response to Inquiry 84.

Subject: Oh it was a *nerve-wracking period of time*—for me it was. Because at that point it was like in June that they did the six-month audit. And there hadn't been a lot of funds taken at that point. It was just very, very little. And I was *a nervous wreck, literally*. But they came in, did all the checks and balances that a midterm audit was supposed to be doing. And then *they never asked any questions*. They … I don't know that they just didn't pull the right checks to check. Because they would go through and pick certain checks and then do and audit. Do a test, what they called them and never caught anything that was out of kilter at that time, even though there had been some crime already committed.

Connect the first two highlighted phrases with the third explaining the advantages to and cautions for the interviewer.

Interviewing Inquiry 85

Interviewer: No one interviewed you? No one sat down and talked with you? They just did the audit?

Subject: Yeah, they just came in. They came in and performed a mechanical audit. Of course they interviewed me. They had to ask me questions about this and ask questions about that.

Interviewing Inquiry 86

Interviewer: Tell me about the interview.

Subject: From the audit standpoint they did ask the typical questions: "Is there anything going on within the company that we need to know about?" Of course they did a balance sheet-income statement audit. And they were going through and reconciling all of the reconciliations that had been done. And so the accounts reconciled the balance sheet. All they did was test work and we passed that audit.

> **Teaching Point:** In an audit there should never be "typical questions." The interviewer asking typical questions is simply not in the game. Under no stretch of the imagination would the interview have been seen as typical by the interviewee. He was, in his own words, "a nervous wreck." The astute interviewer should identify the interviewee's mindset within the conduct of the interview and adjust accordingly. When the interview, the interviewee and the questions asked become typical for the interviewer, then the deceptive, guilty, or guilty knowledge interviewee will "typically" prevail.

Interviewing Inquiry 87

Interviewer: How were you feeling when they were interviewing you and asking you those questions?

Subject: It was a miserable time for me because I ... at that period of time ... I was still ... I was angry with them and really thought it ... part of it was justification for what I was doing. But at the same time I was a nervous wreck. I knew that if I ever got in trouble again because I had the first crime that I had committed. Basically what they had done with that was to listen to the judge. He said he was going to put this in a drawer and leave it there. And if I never ever did anything wrong again it would stay in a drawer. But I knew if I ever got caught doing something like that again ... In the back of my mind I don't know why I did it. But if I got caught I knew I was going to get in very, very serious trouble.

Exercise 3: In the interviewee's response to Inquiry 87, he states that he "was angry with them," "part of it was justification for what I was doing," and "at the same time I was a nervous wreck." Explain how these stated emotions and rationales can be woven together by the interviewer to carry the interview forward to a productive conclusion.

Interviewing Inquiry 88

Interviewer: During the time that the auditor was interviewing you and talking to you did it ever cross your mind, "Do they know something?"

Subject: During the first audit?

Interviewing Inquiry 89

Interviewer: Yes.

Subject: No. Not at all. It did not ... because the amounts were so small at that time—we are talking from the first of May 'til June, Okay? I just really didn't think that the size of that coming about was going to be found. Because it just wouldn't have raised a flag. The amounts were so small.

Teaching Point: The response to Inquiry 89 serves to underscore the importance of the interview during an audit (we never label an audit as routine) or a fraud-related inquiry. It may very well be, as noted in this case, that the audit or the inquiry did not reveal any evidence of fraud. However, asserting, "The audit/inquiry did not reveal any evidence of fraud" is not the same as affirming, "The audit/inquiry revealed evidence of *no fraud*." (You might want to read that last part once more slowly, thinking about each word.) The two statements may sound similar linguistically, but they are miles—more than miles, horizons—apart philosophically.

The audit/inquiry looks to see if someone has been "cooking the books." The interview looks at the "cook." The audit/inquiry may indicate all is copacetic, however, that is only part of the examination. The interview is the other, critical ingredient. It may very well be if the fraud-related interview is conducted at higher levels, the most revealing information may come from the interviewee—the cook.

Interviewing Inquiry 90

Interviewer: If they had randomly pulled one of your checks and placed it on the table, what would have happened?

Subject: Uh … I don't know what I would have done.

Interviewing Inquiry 91

Interviewer: Let's imagine that was the case.

Subject: Okay.

Teaching Point: Inquiry 91 provides an example of an interviewing technique which may be of benefit to you. The following can serve as an illustration. You are conducting an interview and you ask the question, "If someone were going to divert monies out of the operation how could they go about doing it?" The interviewee answers, "I don't have any idea." Try responding with, "Let's imagine that you do." As you can see in Inquiry 91, it gives the interviewee license to imagine; to pretend. The suspension of reality allows the interviewee's imagination to flow and can serve to overcome the inhibitions he or she may have of speculating on reality. Once you respond with "Let's imagine that you do," be prepared for a little quiet time as the interviewee transitions from reality (such as it is) to fantasy land. There can be a short line at the entrance, so be patient and wait for the interviewee to speak first.

Interviewing Inquiry 92

Interviewer: And I am saying, "David, can you tell me about this check for $5,000?"

Subject: There would have been no way I would have had an answer. I would have said, "No, I can't tell you about it."

Interviewing Inquiry 93

Interviewer: Okay.

Subject: And we would have gone from there. See that's the stupidity about it. Because if you think about ... if they had of pulled that check ... I would have had no answer. Now, knowing what I would have known at that time, I would probably have come up with something. I don't know if you would call it BS but I would have tried to BS my way through what it represented. But I don't know from that point what I would have done.

A job related interview that is challenging for me is one where the individual I am interviewing is older and has more experience than me. As a state auditor, I am the one conducting the interview and I may receive resistance to answer questions or someone may question my ability to conduct the interview because I am younger.

—Anonymous class participant

Interviewing Inquiry 94

Interviewer: Let's say you were able to BS your way through that first check.

Subject: Yeah

Interviewing Inquiry 95

Interviewer: And then they pull another check.

Subject: Yeah.

Interviewing Inquiry 96

Interviewer: I know you hadn't written a lot by the time of the first audit, but would you have tried to do it again?

Subject: I would have tried my best to have gotten through that.

Teaching Point: Once again, read what the second fraudster related with regard to responding to an inquiry:

Subject: What I did the first time was I doubled my payroll. Okay, and I had an easy answer for that if I got caught right away. I would say, "It was just a mistake and I am going to fix it on the next payroll." So that was my excuse and that was my reasoning how I did this—how I committed this fraud the first time. I had just started three months prior so I wasn't due for a raise. I think I felt—putting myself back in those shoes—I wanted to give my kids and my family everything they needed material-wise. I wasn't thinking from a mental standpoint, from a physical being standpoint. I wanted to give them everything they needed, toys, stuffed animals, anything they wanted. I wasn't looking at the physical self of being with your children.

Whether it is, as described by the first subject, "BS," or as the second subject related, "an easy answer," at the very bottom it is deception. As you begin to probe with additional questions into specific areas, ask for more and more details. Unless the interviewee is prepared to tell the truth, he or she will have to resort to deception. In the fraud-related interview, do not hesitate to inquire about the details in the details in the details.

This is the point in the interview wherein the information gleaned prior to the interview as well as during the conduct of the interview combine to increasingly strengthen the interviewer's management of the interview process.

Interviewing Inquiry 97

Interviewer: Let's say there were three or four of them.

Subject: No. I think if they had of found that it would have been over.

Interviewing Inquiry 98

Interviewer: That would have done it?

Subject: Yeah. Because the external audit company that was doing the auditing for us was a very reputable company. And if they would have found some impropriety they would have blown it all up. I really do think that.

Explore the Details in the Details in the Details

Teaching Point: Inquiries 90–98 provide an excellent example regarding the presentation of facts, details, or evidence on the part of the interviewer. At this phase of the interview, the interviewer should be thinking in terms of three. Three is the magic number in interviewing. This trio could be comprised of linguistic deception, clues, or mistakes to be addressed with:

- additional questions requiring explanation;

- documentation which disagrees with what the interviewee has asserted previously; and

- contradictory statements from others during the conduct of the interview.

The interviewer should make an effort to ensure he or she has at least three elements (issues or documents) before transitioning to the phase of the interview wherein he or she endeavors to seek an admission from the interviewee. As the interviewee noted, with checks one and two he would have attempted to "BS" his way through. However, the third check served as the tipping point that would have caused him to fold and throw in the cards.

Exercise 4: Read the following.

A 41-year-old woman has been charged with taking $30,000. It has been reported that she made unauthorized credit card purchases and wrote company checks to herself to carry out the embezzlement.

You are responsible for conducting the interview. In your preparation consider:

- What documentary evidence will you have in hand prior to conducting the interview?
- How will you plan to utilize the documentary evidence during the conduct of the interview?
- When will you present the documentary evidence during the conduct of the interview?

Interviewing Inquiry 99

Interviewer: David, you are obviously a nice guy. I can tell you are a nice guy. And you did not commit a crime that involved much in the way of sophistication. You wrote checks to yourself and you deposited them in your own account.

Personable Does Not Automatically Equal Honest

Teaching Point: People who commit fraud tend to be "nice guys" (men and women). That is not the only reason interviewers themselves should be "nice guys" too but it is an important reason. Fraudsters can range from the heretofore honest individual faced with a personal crisis (not necessarily financial in nature) which precipitates the fraud, to the predatory person who commits fraud because that is who they are and what they do. But the commonality between the two extremes is the fraud triangle. For the first person, the pressure/motive which precipitated the fraud may be a once-in-a-lifetime experience. For the second individual, pressure/motive may be the result of a life-long experience. In either case, opportunity and rationalization are there to complete the formula. People respond to "nice." The interviewer who can be nice is a capable, competent interviewer who can objectify — not personalize — the situation in an understanding, nonjudgmental manner. You must endeavor to be that "nice guy."

Subject: It was so simple that is probably why it slipped through. But at the same time, the proper checks and balances put in would have stopped any of this. I should not … as president of the company I should not have check-signing authority. I should not have the authority without some kind of checks and balances of someone else having to sign that check with me that reports not directly to me. Because even if I had a second person, I could have taken the check in and said, "Sign this. We have got to do this."

Interviewing Inquiry 100

Interviewer: Okay.

Subject: And most likely they would have done it. See you need that checks and balances within a company. A president or the controller of the company has no business signing checks for that company.

Interviewing Inquiry 101

Interviewer: So if you were going to help a company put in a proactive policy and procedure those would be some of the things you would have in your policy and procedure—that the auditor would ensure this is not happening among other things?

Subject: Absolutely. Yes exactly

Interviewing Inquiry 102

Interviewer: In looking back—I mean we are all human. As the Bible says, "We have all fallen short."

Subject: Yes.

Interviewing Inquiry 103

Interviewer: If you look back and said, "If I was going to do something wrong again" and I believe that you don't want to do that .

Subject: Never again.

Interviewing Inquiry 104

Interviewer: Have you ever thought, "This is how I would do it in a manner that was more sophisticated?"

Subject: You are going down that route that people that do it get into. There is no way that someone is not going to get caught.

Interviewing Inquiry 105

Interviewer: You think?

Subject: I do not think that anybody, long term, is going to get away with it. Eventually they are either going to get caught up in it their own self; do something that someone is going to see wrong— or companies ... the accounting systems that are in ... balances that are in are going to eventually catch someone. I don't think anyone is smart enough ever to propriate (*sic*) a crime and continue propriating (*sic*) it and not eventually get caught. I don't ... I don't think there is anything I can go back and say, "Okay. If I had done this, this would not have happened." You have to imagine during those eight months in jail, I went through those things: "Why did I do this? Why did I do that?" Because it was so stupid! I mean I could have done this different. I would have done that different. But it is really not about that. The healing process that I went through was about saying "Nothing you can do is going to keep you from getting caught. You are eventually going to get caught."

Interviewing Inquiry 106

Interviewer: While you are with Company B and once you get past the initial audit. Every day you get up and look in the mirror, you shave and do you think to yourself, "I am a thief"? Do you think to yourself, "If they had treated me right in the first place this would not have been necessary"? What do you think during the course of your day?

Subject: I do think sometimes ... but not now ... I did. I have gone through a lot of healing. And I have done a lot of mind searching. I don't think that anything justifies what I did. I agreed to a salary ... agreed to a job. This is what the requirements are, you do it. Now that is where I am at with that attitude about they owed me more money. I agreed to the salary. When I look at my resume that is all that resume demanded on the market. All I could have made. For me thinking that a guy with three years experience in this industry should be making the $250,000 that that guy having twenty-five years in that industry was making was ludicrous. Now should there have been a happy medium? In my head I think there should have been a happy medium. But it doesn't justify what I did.

Exercise 5: Summarize the lessons learned from the inquiries and the responses in Inquiries 66–106.

Examination: Chapter 7

What possibilities could there be for the person at Company B who reconciled the checks *not* to report the interviewee, as opposed to the person in Company A who *did* report the fraud?

    1. _____

    2. _____

How would you conduct a fraud-related interview with the administrative assistant who reconciled the checks at Company B?

    3. _____

    4. _____

What was the interviewee's mental state while being interviewed by the auditor after he had begun his fraudulent activity?

    5. _____

    6. _____

Describe the benefits of being able to suspend reality in the mind of the interviewee during the conduct of the interview.

    7. _____

    8. _____

    9. _____

   10. _____

Chapter 8

Capability

The Fraud Diamond

There are those who subscribe to the theory wherein the fraud diagram is not a triangle, but a diamond. In this instance, pressure/motive, opportunity, and rationalization comprise the left point, top, and right point of the diamond, respectively. The bottom point of the diamond is labeled "capability."

Capability is to be defined as:

1. the quality of being capable; capacity; ability: His capability was unquestionable.
2. the ability to undergo or be affected by a given treatment or action.(Dictionary.com)

Those subscribing to this concept assert that it is possible for all three primary elements—pressure/motive, opportunity and rationalization—to be present, but that the individual does not have the capacity to commit the fraud. For these theorists:

- the pressure/motive may be profound in the individual's life;
- the opportunity to commit the fraud may be directly in front of him or her; and
- the individual may justify the commission of the fraud.

Yet given all three dynamics, the individual simply is not capable of bringing him- or herself to commit the fraud. Both authors, having been law enforcement officers, conceptualize this as follows. Two individuals could have gone through the same law enforcement training, have the same equipment, the same on-the-job experience, the same skill level in marksmanship, are versed in the law with regard to the use of deadly force, and now find themselves together in a life-or-death situation justifying the use of deadly force. In this example, the pressure/motive is there—it is the life-or-death situation. Opportunity is there—each officer has a weapon and the justification to use deadly force. Rationalization is there—save your life or the life of your partner. Yet given all of that, the question remains, "Is the individual capable of pulling the weapon out, aiming it at another human being, and pulling the trigger to save their own life or the life of their partner?" Obviously only when a person is placed into the actual situation as described would the question be answered, and hopefully to the safety of the officers involved.

However, the shoot-don't shoot capability of the officers in question can only be demonstrated in relation to the specific, articulated criteria. Change the criteria and the capability question may be answered differently. In one situation the individual threatening the life of the officers may be an 11-year-old. In another case the life that the officer has the opportunity to save may be his or her own child. The variety of permutations is endless with each containing the potential for a different response on the part of the officer involved.

Now back to the potential fraudster. Our position is "capability" in this circumstance is also a sliding scale, for example, a given set of circumstances such as when the pressure/motive and rationalization levels for the individual are low is not enough to require fraudulent activity to return control to a life perceived as out of control. In this situation, an individual may not have the *capability* to commit the fraud. However, by continuing to raise the intensity of the pressure/motive and rationalization elements, there exists an increased possibility for a tipping point at which an individual would be capable of committing fraud. Of course we would never truly know unless we tried every circumstance on every human being, but it is not necessary to do so. Earlier in the text we asked, "Would you steal if your children were starving?" We think it safe to say that most parents would steal to feed their starving children. Consequently, in theory, there is a tipping point, a line in the sand over which the vast majority of people, having crossed it, would become fraudsters. The only question that remains is, "where is the line for a given individual?"

As the definition articulates, an individual is capable when he or she has become "affected by a given treatment or action." The treatment or action in this case is the right combination of pressure/motive, opportunity and rationalization. The outcome of being so affected is the commission of fraud. Consequently, in reality the element "capability" is the end product of the first three ingredients.

The situation-specific fraudster is an individual whose life intersects with the opportunity to steal. There is no pressure/motive element setting the stage for the commission of fraud. With the situation-specific fraudster, it could well be said that the opportunity index level increased for whatever reason—finding a signed check, a deposit bag filled with cash, discovery of operational weaknesses, a bribe from a vendor, and so on—was such that it resulted in the individual having the capacity to commit the fraud. It may be simply in a moment of weakness that the person succumbed to temptation.

For the predatory fraudster, the interviewer must think a little more long-term. His or her proclivity to commit fraud may be a result of a lifetime of experiences. And while we will leave the psychoanalysis of these individuals to those with more time on their hands, it remains important to note the big three—pressure/motive, opportunity, and rationalization—have resulted in an individual having the capability for committing fraud. The genesis of a predatory fraudster's pressure/motive or rationalization may go back years or decades and have been and are being projected on situation after situation—fraud after fraud.

For the fraud-related interview, it all comes down to this: There is an individual sitting across from you. The individual may or may not have committed the fraud. You do know, however, in the right combination of pressure/motive, opportunity, and rationalization, that the individual is most likely to become capable of committing fraud. Audits and investigations provide tributaries of information flowing into your interview. Your interview may in all likelihood flow to further inquiries and investigations. And so it goes. Your task is to engage an interviewee in such a manner he or she will "undergo or be affected by a given treatment or action." Your conduct of the interview results in the truth being made known.

When interviewing the fraudster, you must become the pressure/motive, opportunity, and rationalization in the interviewee's life. The pressure/motive element involves your fraud-related interviewing knowledge, skills, and abilities engaging the individual to respond. The opportunity element relates to your ability to understand the interviewee as they reveal themselves to you. The rationalization element relates to your ability to convince the interviewee that compliance is the best course of action. By using the three elements appropriately, the interviewer transitions the interviewee into an individual with the capability to tell the truth.

Conclusion

While we may rightfully think of ourselves as interviewer diamonds in the rough, we should continue to polish and smooth our interviewing abilities, all the while remembering that a diamond starts as a lump of coal which is then placed under a great deal of pressure. As fraud-related interviewers, our pressure/motive should provide us with the desire to improve continually. Every interview makes available an opportunity to learn and improve. Our rationale is that the interview is too important to be typical. Last, we believe that through practice, we will be more capable tomorrow than we are today.

Appendix A

Chapter 1:
Before We Get Started

Application Question 1: What effect, if any, do you believe the initial moments of the fraud-related interview has on the overall conduct and ultimate success of the interview?

Application Question 2: What preparation do you undertake for the first few moments of the interview?

Application Question 3: Have you ever conducted an interview wherein you could tell from the first few moments the interview would go well? How did you know?

Application Question 4: Have you ever conducted an interview wherein you could tell from the first few moments the interview would go poorly? How did you know?

Application Question 5: If someone were to ask you to tell them about yourself, how would you describe yourself?

Application Question 6: In the following response, how did the interviewee describe himself?

> **Subject:** Basically, I was raised, was born in Winston-Salem, North Carolina but my family moved when I was like six years old to Charleston, South Carolina. So that's been where I was basically raised. Of course my mom and dad are still living. I've got two siblings that are still living. I have children. They all still live there in Winston. I went to high school in Winston-Salem. Graduated from high school. Went to a local

community college one year. Met my wife, my first wife Marie, at the community college. We transferred after that first year to the University of North Carolina. Where she got her business management degree and I got a degree in finance. From there I've got four children, Mary, Susan, Helen, and Sandra. They live with their mother still in Winston-Salem. And that is a quick version of who I am and where I'm from.

Application Question 7: Who was mentioned in the description?

Subject: Basically, I was raised, was born in Winston-Salem, North Carolina but my family moved when I was like six years old to Charleston, South Carolina. So that's been where I was basically raised. Of course my mom and dad are still living. I've got two siblings that are still living. I have children. They all still live there in Winston. I went to high school in Winston-Salem. Graduated from high school. Went to a local community college one year. Met my wife, my first wife Marie, at the community college. We transferred after that first year to the University of North Carolina. Where she got her business management degree and I got a degree in finance. From there I've got four children, Mary, Susan, Helen, and Sandra. They live with their mother still in Winston-Salem. And that is a quick version of who I am and where I'm from.

Application Question 8: How were the relationships articulated?

Subject: Basically, I was raised, was born in Winston-Salem, North Carolina but my family moved when I was like six years old to Charleston, South Carolina. So that's been where I was basically raised. Of course my mom and dad are still living. I've got two siblings that are still living. I have children. They all still live there in Winston. I went to high school in Winston-Salem. Graduated from high school. Went to a local community college one year. Met my wife, my first wife Marie, at the community college. We transferred after that first year to the University of North Carolina. Where she got her business management degree and I got a degree in finance. From there I've got four children, Mary, Susan, Helen, and San-dra. They live with their mother still in Winston-Salem. And that is a quick version of who I am and where I'm from.

Application Question 9: From his overall self-description, what impression do you have?

Subject: Basically, I was raised, was born in Winston-Salem, North Carolina but my family moved when I was like six years old to Charleston, South Carolina. So that's been where I was basically raised. Of course my mom and dad are still living. I've got two siblings that are still living. I have children. They all still live there in Winston. I went to high school in Win-ston-Salem. Graduated from high school. Went to a local community college one year. Met my wife, my first wife Marie, at the community college. We transferred after that first year to the University of North Carolina. Where she got her busi-ness management degree and I got a degree in finance. From there I've got four children, Mary, Susan, Helen, and San-dra. They live with their mother still in Winston-Salem. And that is a quick version of who I am and where I'm from.

Application Question 10: What is revealed by the key phrase, "a quick version of who I am," in the last sentence of the interviewee's self-description?

Subject: Basically, I was raised, was born in Winston-Salem, North Carolina but my family moved when I was like six years old to Charleston, South Carolina. So that's been where I was basically raised. Of course my mom and dad are still living. I've got two siblings that are still living. I have children. They all still live there in Winston. I went to high school in Win-ston-Salem. Graduated from high school. Went to a local community college one year. Met my wife, my first wife Marie, at the community college. We transferred after that first year to the University of North Carolina. Where she got her busi-ness management degree and I got a degree in finance. From there I've got four children, Mary, Susan, Helen, and Sandra. They live with their mother still in Winston-Salem. And that is a quick version of who I am and where I'm from.

Application Question 11: In what context regarding others does the interviewee describe himself?

Subject: I was born and raised in Atlanta, Georgia. Grew up there. My family was probably as dysfunctional as they come and I don't want to brag about that. My parents were divorced when I was three years old. My mother was having medical problems. I lived with my father. I had an older brother and two older sisters. I was kind of the baby of the family. My next youngest sister was nine years older than I was. I guess I realized that … back in the beginning when I was born or maybe five, six, seven years old, that I had the ability to talk my way out of things … a knack for … a knack … I use that word knack. A knack for being able to talk my way out of anything. If I ever got in trouble in school; if I ever got in trouble with my grandparents I was always able to talk my way out of it. It was kind of tough growing up. My father was in the bakery business. My grandfather was in the bakery business. They really didn't get along too well. Unfortunately I was in the middle. So that basically … I guess you would say that I came from a broken home.

Application Question 12: What interview strategy adjustments, if any, would you undertake when the interviewee articulates he has learned he has the ability "to talk my way out of anything"?

Subject: I was born and raised in Atlanta, Georgia. Grew up there. My family was probably as dysfunctional as they come and I don't want to brag about that. My parents were divorced when I was three years old. My mother was having medical problems. I lived with my father. I had an older brother and two older sisters. I was kind of the baby of the family. My next youngest sister was nine years older than I was. I guess I realized that … back in the beginning when I was born or maybe five, six, seven years old that I had the ability to talk my way out of things … a knack for … a knack … I use that word knack. A knack for being able to talk my way out of anything. If I ever got in trouble in school; if I ever got in trouble with my grandparents I was always able to talk my way out of it. It was kind of tough growing up. My father was in the bakery business. My grandfather was in the bakery business. They really didn't get along too well. Unfortunately I was in the middle. So that basically … I guess you would say that I came from a broken home.

Application Question 13: What would be your connecting response to this interviewee as it applies to the preceding question?

Application Question 14: What are the salient points raised in the interviewee's description of himself?

Subject: I was born and raised in Atlanta, Georgia. Grew up there. My family was probably as dysfunctional as they come and I don't want to brag about that. My parents were divorced when I was three years old. My mother was having medical problems. I lived with my father. I had an older brother and two older sisters. I was kind of the baby of the family. My next youngest sister was nine years older than I was. I guess I realized that … back in the beginning when I was born or maybe five, six, seven years old that I had the ability to talk my way out of things … a knack for … a knack … I use that word knack. A knack for being able to talk my way out of anything. If I ever got in trouble in school; if I ever got in trouble with my grandparents I was always able to talk my way out of it. It was kind of tough growing up. My father was in the bakery business. My grandfather was in the bakery business. They really didn't get along too well. Unfortunately I was in the middle. So that basically … I guess you would say that I came from a broken home.

Application Question 15: How would you formulate a question with regard to his mother's medical problems?

Subject: I was born and raised in Atlanta, Georgia. Grew up there. My family was probably as dysfunctional as they come and I don't want to brag about that. My parents were divorced when I was three years old. My mother was having medical problems. I lived with my father. I had an older brother and two older sisters. I was kind of the baby of the family. My next youngest sister was nine years older than I was. I guess I realized that ... back in the beginning when I was born or maybe five, six, seven years old that I had the ability to talk my way out of things ... a knack for ... a knack ... I use that word knack. A knack for being able to talk my way out of anything. If I ever got in trouble in school; if I ever got in trouble with my grandparents I was always able to talk my way out of it. It was kind of tough growing up. My father was in the bakery business. My grandfather was in the bakery business. They really didn't get along too well. Unfortunately I was in the middle. So that basically ... I guess you would say that I came from a broken home.

Application Question 16: How would you formulate a question with regard to the divorce of his parents?

Subject: I was born and raised in Atlanta, Georgia. Grew up there. My family was probably as dysfunctional as they come and I don't want to brag about that. My parents were divorced when I was three years old. My mother was having medical problems. I lived with my father. I had an older brother and two older sisters. I was kind of the baby of the family. My next youngest sister was nine years older than I was. I guess I realized that ... back in the beginning when I was born or maybe five, six, seven years old that I had the ability to talk my way out of things ... a knack for ... a knack ... I use that word knack. A knack for being able to talk my way out of anything. If I ever got in trouble in school; if I ever got in trouble with my grandparents I was always able to talk my way out of it. It was kind of tough growing up. My father was in the bakery business. My grandfather was in the bakery business. They really didn't get along too well. Unfortunately I was in the middle. So that basically … I guess you would say that I came from a broken home.

Application Question 17: How would you formulate a question with regard to his siblings?

Subject: I was born and raised in Atlanta, Georgia. Grew up there. My family was probably as dysfunctional as they come and I don't want to brag about that. My parents were divorced when I was three years old. My mother was having medical problems. I lived with my father. I had an older brother and two older sisters. I was kind of the baby of the family. My next youngest sister was nine years older than I was. I guess I realized that … back in the beginning when I was born or maybe five, six, seven years old that I had the ability to talk my way out of things … a knack for … a knack … I use that word knack. A knack for being able to talk my way out of anything. If I ever got in trouble in school; if I ever got in trouble with my grandparents I was always able to talk my way out of it. It was kind of tough growing up. My father was in the bakery business. My grandfather was in the bakery business. They really didn't get along too well. Unfortunately I was in the middle. So that basically … I guess you would say that I came from a broken home.

Application Question 18: How would you formulate a question with regard to the conflict between his father and grandfather and his being caught in the middle?

Subject: I was born and raised in Atlanta, Georgia. Grew up there. My family was probably as dysfunctional as they come and I don't want to brag about that. My parents were divorced when I was three years old. My mother was having medical problems. I lived with my father. I had an older brother and two older sisters. I was kind of the baby of the family. My next youngest sister was nine years older than I was. I guess I realized that … back in the beginning when I was born or maybe five, six, seven years old that I had the ability to talk my way out of things ... a knack for ... a knack ... I use that word knack. A knack for being able to talk my way out of anything. If I ever got in trouble in school; if I ever got in trouble with my grandparents I was always able to talk my way out of it. It was kind of tough growing up. My father was in the bakery business. My grandfather was in the bakery business. They really didn't get along too well. Unfortunately I was in the middle. So that basically ... I guess you would say that I came from a broken home.

Application Question 19: How would you formulate a question with regard to his description of his family as dysfunctional?

Subject: I was born and raised in Atlanta, Georgia. Grew up there. My family was probably as dysfunctional as they come and I don't want to brag about that. My parents were divorced when I was three years old. My mother was having medical problems. I lived with my father. I had an older brother and two older sisters. I was kind of the baby of the family. My next youngest sister was nine years older than I was. I guess I realized that ... back in the beginning when I was born or maybe five, six, seven years old that I had the ability to talk my way out of things ... a knack for ... a knack ... I use that word knack. A knack for being able to talk my way out of anything. If I ever got in trouble in school; if I ever got in trouble with my grandparents I was always able to talk my way out of it. It was kind of tough growing up. My father was in the bakery business. My grandfather was in the bakery business. They really didn't get along too well. Unfortunately I was in the middle. So that basically ... I guess you would say that I came from a broken home.

Application Question 20: Why would Application Questions 14–18 be appropriate at this stage of the interview process?

Application Question 21: What insight into the interviewee is revealed from his statement that he does not want to "brag" about the dysfunctional status of his family?

Subject: I was born and raised in Atlanta, Georgia. Grew up there. My family was probably as dysfunctional as they come and I don't want to brag about that. My parents were divorced when I was three years old. My mother was having medical problems. I lived with my father. I had an older brother and two older sisters. I was kind of the baby of the family. My next youngest sister was nine years older than I was. I guess I realized that … back in the beginning when I was born or maybe five, six, seven years old that I had the ability to talk my way out of things … a knack for … a knack … I use that word knack. A knack for being able to talk my way out of anything. If I ever got in trouble in school; if I ever got in trouble with my grandparents I was always able to talk my way out of it. It was kind of tough growing up. My father was in the bakery business. My grandfather was in the bakery business. They really didn't get along too well. Unfortunately I was in the middle. So that basically … I guess you would say that I came from a broken home.

Exercise 1: Write down the salient points of the interviewee's self-description as illustrated from the following narrative.

Subject: Basically, I was raised, was born in Winston-Salem, North Carolina but my family moved when I was like six years old to Charleston, South Carolina. So that's been where I was basically raised. Of course my mom and dad are still living. I've got two siblings that are still living. I have children. They all still live there in Winston. I went to high school in Winston-Salem. Graduated from high school. Went to a local community college one year. Met my wife, my first wife Marie, at the community college. We transferred after that first year to the University of North Carolina. Where she got her business management degree and I got a degree in finance. From there I've got four children, Mary, Susan, Helen, and Sandra. They live with their mother still in Winston-Salem. And that is a quick version of who I am and where I'm from.

Exercise 2: Write an open question for each identified interviewee self-descriptive element.

Subject: Basically, I was raised, was born in Winston-Salem, North Carolina but my family moved when I was like six years old to Charleston, South Carolina. So that's been where I was basically raised. Of course my mom and dad are still living. I've got two siblings that are still living. I have children. They all still live there in Winston. I went to high school in Winston-Salem. Graduated from high school. Went to a local community college one year. Met my wife, my first wife Marie, at the community college. We transferred after that first year to the University of North Carolina. Where she got her business management degree and I got a degree in finance. From there I've got four children, Mary, Susan, Helen, and Sandra. They live with their mother still in Winston-Salem. And that is a quick version of who I am and where I'm from.

Exercise 3: Based on what the interviewee has shared about himself in the following narrative, identify and write down five responses that you could have employed if you had been the interviewer.

Subject: Basically, I was raised, was born in Winston-Salem, North Carolina but my family moved when I was like six years old to Charleston, South Carolina. So that's been where I was basically raised. Of course my mom and dad are still living. I've got two siblings that are still living. I have children. They all still live there in Winston. I went to high school in Winston-Salem. Graduated from high school. Went to a local community college one year. Met my wife, my first wife Marie, at the community college. We transferred after that first year to the University of North Carolina. Where she got her business management degree and I got a degree in finance. From there I've got four children, Mary, Susan, Helen, and Sandra. They live with their mother still in Winston-Salem. And that is a quick version of who I am and where I'm from.

Appendix B

Chapter 2: Pressure/Motive: Company A

Application Question 1: Have you ever been placed in a situation wherein it would have been possible for you to convert money or other material to your own use? If so, what were those circumstances?

Application Question 2: Even for just a fleeting moment, did you ever think about doing that very thing?

Application Question 3: Could a circumstance, any circumstance, ever arise that would result in you converting money or other material belonging to others to yourself?

Application Question 4: If your children were starving, would you steal?

Application Question 5: In the interviewee's response in Inquiry 6, what is his pressure/motive?

Interviewing Inquiry 6

Interviewer: [Take me all the way] from the very beginning of your criminal activity to the end as far as that particular company is concerned.

Subject: Okay. The way it basically got started was I had started an extramarital affair. And I was in the process of moving out of the home and moving to another city. And from that point on, during my work there we were in a growing time for the company. We were real busy and then as it did happen I got short on funds. Because here I was living two lives. And the opportunity came and presented itself for me to commit the fraud that I committed. I basically started and I wrote a check to myself. I had check-signing responsibilities with one of the other officers there at the company. And with the human resources director too. And as long as there were two signatures the checks would go through. I wrote one check to myself, deposited it into my bank there in town. Literally went through funds very, very rapidly. Through materiality, blowing money, blowing funds. And that perpetrated me doing another check. I wrote two checks to myself out of that company. Signed them and deposited them directly into my bank account.

Application Question 6: What were the consequences of his pressure/motive?

Exercise 1: Compare the phrases "living two lives" and "that is a quick version of who I am" found in Inquiries 1–3 located in Chapter 1. Together, these phrases provide greater insight into the interviewee. The consummate interviewer must understand the interviewee has multiple versions involving self and develop an understanding attitude. Honestly reflect on your own ability to nonjudgmentally accept the various versions of pressure/motive presented by those who sit across from you.

Interviewing Inquiry 1

Interviewer: David, before we get started, if you will tell me about yourself.

Subject: Basically, I was raised, was born in Winston-Salem, North Carolina but my family moved when I was like six years old to Charleston, South Carolina. So that's been where I was basically raised. Of course my mom and dad are still living. I've got two siblings that are still living. I have children. They all still live there in Winston. I went to high school in Winston-Salem. Graduated from high school. Went to a local community college one year. Met my wife, my first wife, Marie, at the community college. We transferred after that first year to the University of North Carolina. Where she got her business management degree and I got a degree in finance. From there I've got four children, Mary, Susan, Helen, and Sandra. They live with their mother still in Winston-Salem. And that is a quick version of who I am and where I'm from.

Interviewing Inquiry 2

Interviewer: Where is Charleston in relationship to Greenville?

Subject: To Greenville? Greenville is in the northwest corner. It's actually a drive of several hours if you take the interstate route from Charleston.

Interviewing Inquiry 3

Interviewer: I've been to Charleston and also to Winston-Salem a number of times.

Subject: Okay.

Application Question 7: What was the interviewee's articulated pressure/motive?

Subject: I have a wife who stays home with my two daughters. I wanted the best for them. I guess I was willing to do whatever it took to make sure they had whatever they wanted. If they wanted $200 worth of toys at Toys R Us, they didn't have to ask for it. I look back at the way that I was raised and my family ... my grandfather had seven bakeries in the Midwest and I never really needed anything. And I wanted to be that kind of person.

Application Question 8: How did the interviewee describe the circumstances of his own childhood with how he wanted to be perceived by his wife and daughters?

Subject: I have a wife who stays home with my two daughters. I wanted the best for them. I guess I was willing to do whatever it took to make sure they had whatever they wanted. If they wanted $200 worth of toys at Toys R Us, they didn't have to ask for it. I look back at the way that I was raised and my family ... my grandfather had seven bakeries in the Midwest and I never really needed anything. And I wanted to be that kind of person.

Exercise 2: A company has determined there is a $9.9 million shortage on the books. The woman (Jane) to be interviewed has served as the company's chief financial officer for the last six years. Because she is such a trusted employee, the company has never hired an outside auditor to check the books. Based on the information provided in Chapters 1 and 2, as well as your individual reflections upon the application questions, develop an interview plan in writing for conducting the interview with Jane. Write out the questions you would utilize.

Exercise 3: Recently at an elementary school, a teacher was sued when one of the checks from the Parent-Teacher Association (PTA) bounced. A review of the books revealed a $10,000 shortage. An interview is to be conducted with the former president of the association. She was president from October of one year until June of the following year. She is a mother of three children and had at least one child enrolled at the elementary school during the time she was president of the PTA. At this school, over 80%of the students are on a "meals for free" or "reduced cost" status. Based on the information provided in Chapters 1 and 2, as well as your individual reflections upon the application questions, develop an interview plan in writing for conducting the interview. Write out the questions you would utilize.

Exercise 4: Read the following letter.

From: Jane Doe

To: Tammy Fay

Date: November 7, 2____

Subject: Jump Rope for Health

Tammy Fay,

I received your email from Mrs. _____ yesterday morning about "what happened to the money raised for the Acme Health Association (AHA) at _____ in June 2___". For the past three years I have raised money here at _____school for the AHA. My children have gone to/go to _____ school and I knew that Coach _____ had not done Jump Rope for Health in the past. When I saw that they were going to participate, I asked Coach _____ if she would like some help. She was very appreciative since she had little experience with the whole event. She began giving me the envelopes with checks and money. I had exchanged small bills for large to make room and to be counted. The event took place on a Friday and when it was over I took the rest of the envelopes and finished counting the money. Over the weekend I finished the prize list and counted the money. The day I faxed the list to the AHA is the day I took the prestamped, addressed envelope to the post office on _____ street. Without thinking, I sealed the envelope with everything inside and put it in the mailbox. There was a little less than $800 in cash that I did not get a cashier's check for and the rest were personal checks written to AHA. In all, the total was $6,893. I talked to _____ and _____ (555-123-4567) at the AHA office several times. _____ said that the envelope could have had the old address and may have come back. I went to the post office to see if they had found the envelope, but it was not there. The last time we spoke, she said that when the envelope was put in the mail that it was no longer my responsibility. I went by the post office two times to see if they had ever found the envelope. The envelope is still missing and has not been returned or found. Please let me know what I need to do next. As I said before, I have been doing this for a few years and have never had any trouble.

Jane Doe

Based on the information provided in Chapters 1 and 2 as well as your individual reflections upon the application questions, develop an interview plan in writing for conducting the interview. Write out the questions you would utilize.

Application Question 9: Did you find yourself planning each interview based on the limited facts provided in the same way. What could be the advantages or disadvantages of doing so?

Application Question 10: After completing Exercises 2 and 3, did anything develop in your mind with regard to interviewing persons suspected of fraud? What about after you completed Exercise 4?

Application Question 11: Over time, what negative effect on the mindset of the interviewer do you think could develop after working case after case, audit after audit, and interview after interview?

Application Question 12: What steps do you think an interviewer must take to make sure the negative mindset does not prevail? Have you done, or do you think you could do just that?

Appendix C

Chapter 3:
Opportunity: Company A

Application Question 1: How do you conceptualize *opportunity*?

Application Question 2: Is opportunity something that someone causes to happen or something that happens to someone?

Application Question 3: Are opportunities intrinsically always good?

Application Question 4: Why do you think the interviewee would present the concept of opportunity utilizing the phrasing he did?

Interviewing Inquiry 6

Subject: Okay. The way it basically got started was I had started an extramarital affair.

And I was in the process of moving out of the home and moving to another city. And from that point on, during my work there we were in a growing time for the company. We were real busy and then as it did happen I got short on funds. Because here I was living two lives. And the opportunity came and presented itself for me to commit the fraud that I committed. I basically started and I wrote a check to myself. I had check-signing responsibilities with one of the other officers there at the company. And with the human resources director too. And as long as there were two signatures, the checks would go through. I wrote one check to myself, deposited it into my bank there in town. Literally went through funds very, very rapidly. Through materiality, blowing money, blowing

115

funds. And that perpetrated me doing another check. I wrote two checks to myself out of that company. Signed them and deposited them directly into my bank account.

Application Question 5: What options are placed on the table for the interviewer as a result of the interviewee's opportunity-focused revelation?

Interviewing Inquiry 6

Subject: Okay. The way it basically got started was I had started an extramarital affair.

And I was in the process of moving out of the home and moving to another city. And from that point on, during my work there we were in a growing time for the company. We were real busy and then as it did happen I got short on funds. Because here I was living two lives. And the opportunity came and presented itself for me to commit the fraud that I committed. I basically started and I wrote a check to myself. I had check-signing responsibilities with one of the other officers there at the company. And with the human resources director too. And as long as there were two signatures, the checks would go through. I wrote one check to myself, deposited it into my bank there in town. Literally went through funds very, very rapidly. Through materiality, blowing money, blowing funds. And that perpetrated me doing another check. I wrote two checks to myself out of that company. Signed them and deposited them directly into my bank account.

Application Question 6: How would you contrast the stance of fraudster 2 with regard to opportunity with that of fraudster 1?

Subject Two: Everything was going well at home. I don't know what happened. I can't explain it. One day I saw an opportunity and I took advantage of it. And that opportunity was, when I started one of my jobs as controller was to do the salary payroll. I didn't do the hourly payroll. I had somebody that did the hourly payroll. And I did the salary payroll. And I believe the reason for that is they did not want other people seeing what the managers and the upper management made. So I did the payroll for about ten to twelve people on a biweekly, every other week basis. It was my job to run the checks, to put the payroll and at the end of the month, who do you think reconciled the bank statement? And I think that is pretty common. Every month end I got the bank statement in, nobody else opened it. I opened it, reconciled the bank statement. So I, being the quick thinker that I am—and I guess I look at that as an asset or a liability—I saw an opportunity to take advantage of. Probably three months after I started I decided to try it out.

What I did the first time was I doubled my payroll. Okay, and I had an easy answer for that if I got caught right away. I would say, "It was just a mistake and I am going to fix it on the next payroll." So that was my excuse and that was my reasoning how I did this; how I committed this fraud the first time. I had just started three months prior so I wasn't due for a raise. I think I felt—putting myself back in those shoes—I wanted to give my kids and my family everything they needed material-wise. I wasn't thinking from a mental standpoint, from a physical being standpoint. I wanted to give them everything they needed, toys, stuffed animals, anything they wanted. I wasn't looking at the physical self of being with your children.

Application Question 7: Subject 1 indicated the "opportunity presented itself to me." Subject 2 said "I decided to try it out." From an interviewer's perspective, what is the difference?

Application Question 8: For subject 2, what are the articulated pressure/motive components in his narrative as stated in Application Question 6?

Application Question 9: What questions would you ask to gain an understanding of the phrase "I wasn't thinking from a mental standpoint." from the narrative used in Application Question 6?

Application Question 10: How would you determine the difference in the interviewee's mind between a "mental standpoint" and a "physical being standpoint" from the narrative provided in Application Question 6?

Application Question 11: As an interviewer, why would you even concern yourself with understanding the interviewee's definitions of "mental standpoint" and "physical being standpoint"?

Exercise 1: Read the following.

A 42-year-old soccer mom has been arrested for embezzling $72,000 from the school soccer club for which she was serving a treasurer. The preliminary investigation has revealed she wrote checks to her teenage son and to her landlord.

You are responsible for planning and conducting an interview with this woman.

Interview Preparation Question 1: In developing an interviewing plan, how will you factor in the possibilities regarding pressure/motive in the conduct of the interview?

Exercise 1: Read the following.

A 42-year-old soccer mom has been arrested for embezzling $72,000 from the school soccer club for which she was serving a treasurer. The preliminary investigation has revealed she wrote checks to her teenage son and to her landlord.

You are responsible for planning and conducting an interview with this woman.

Interview Preparation Question 2: In developing an interviewing plan, how will you factor in the concept of opportunity into the conduct of the interview?

Exercise 1: Read the following.

A 42-year-old soccer mom has been arrested for embezzling $72,000 from the school soccer club for which she was serving a treasurer. The preliminary investigation has revealed she wrote checks to her teenage son and to her landlord.

You are responsible for planning and conducting an interview with this woman.

Interview Preparation Question 3: In developing an interviewing plan, how will you utilize the implication that she wrote checks to her teenage son?

Exercise 1: Read the following:

A 42-year-old soccer mom has been arrested for embezzling $72,000 from the school soccer club for which she was serving a treasurer. The preliminary investigation has revealed she wrote checks to her teenage son and to her landlord.

You are responsible for planning and conducting an interview with this woman.

Interview Preparation Question 4: In developing an interviewing plan, how will you utilize the implication that she wrote checks to her landlord?

Appendix D

Chapter 4:
Rationalization: Company A

Application Question 1: Have you even been in a situation wherein you did something you normally would not do?

Application Question 2: Was it something which violated your own sense of right and wrong?

Application Question 3: How did you reconcile your actions in your own mind?

Exercise 1: Let's return to the situation we examined in Chapter 3.

A 42-year-old soccer mom has been arrested for embezzling $72,000 from the school soccer club for which she was serving a treasurer. The preliminary investigation has revealed she wrote checks to her teenage son and to her landlord.

You are responsible for planning and conducting an interview with this woman.

Interview Preparation Question 1: In developing an interviewing plan, how will you factor in the concept of rationalization into the conduct of the interview?

Exercise 1: Let's return to the situation we examined in Chapter 3.

A 42-year-old soccer mom has been arrested for embezzling $72,000 from the school soccer club for which she was serving a treasurer. The preliminary investigation has revealed she wrote checks to her teenage son and to her landlord.

You are responsible for planning and conducting an interview with this woman.

Interview Preparation Question 2: What will be your alternate plan with regard to rationalization?

Application Question 4: Have you ever heard someone assert, "No one understands me"? What do you think they were really saying?

Application Question 5: Has anyone ever said to you, "You just don't understand"?

Application Question 6: If the answer to Application Questions 5 is "yes" what was your response?

Application Question 7: In the response to Question 6, what was the implied pressure/motive?

Application Question 8: What subtle indications of the shifting of responsibility from the interviewee to external factors are presented?

Application Question 9: How could an interviewer utilize these shifts to gain compliance from the interviewee?

Application Question 10: What does the interviewee's reflective observation about himself reveal? *"But I have always been very successful at the jobs I've done so my success kind of overshadowed anything they thought might have been going on."*

Exercise 2: Using the information found in the following narrative regarding missing money, develop an interview plan which incorporates the information in Chapters 1–4 (opening, pressure/motive, opportunity, rationalization) following the FRAUD acronym format:

> *Sunday morning started out smooth. I came in at about 7:45 to open. I found a note from my mother from the night before that said that she left the money that I need to open with on the top of the bags. I opened the safe about 10:10. Got the money and put it in the register. I closed and set the safe on day lock and began to open the store. About 11:45 Mary Smith (owner) came in and dropped off some stuff. I went about finishing up my work with dishes. When I got some customers 6–7, 13:50–13:80. The back door was not closed and during me making the sandwiches the safe was opened and most to all the money was removed. I notice at about 13:85 that the safe had been opened and called the owner to see if she had taken the money. She said no and told me to call the police and ask the people up front if they had seen anyone in the back room. I never got straight answer from them.*

Exercise 3: Do the same with the following two narratives from the same individual. Include in your plan the sequencing of who you would interview as well as the interviewing FRAUD format for each interviewee:

> *"I, Susan _____ closed Acme General at 8 pm on 4-27-_____. Patty _____ and myself finished checking out people at about 8:30. At this time, I started taking down the registers. As we arrived at the back door going into the stock room we both heard a noise. I put the registers into the office and closed and locked the office door. At this time we both looked around the store and under the clothes. We saw nothing. She finished cleaning and straightening the store, I was in the back office finishing the bank deposits and counting the drawers down. As I was finishing up Patty sat down at the break table to wait on me. When I finished I ask Patty if she had ever helped anyone hide the money. She said, "Yes a long time ago." So I ask her to help carry the roll*

change, and she did. We then walked to the office to get my things
when I remember to latch the back door and put the bar up. I
then walked down to the breaker box and cut off the lights. We
both then walked to the front of the store. We unlocked the door
and we went out. I relocked the door and we went to the bank.
Patty went her way and I went home.

4-30-20__

    I left my house at 7:30 am and went to pick up Jane _____.
We went to McDonalds to get a cup of coffee but their comput-
ers were down. They said it would be about 30 minutes. So we
went across the street to the Pantry. We both got a cup of coffee
and I bought a pack of cigarettes. We went to Acme General
where we saw Julie waiting for us — Martie, Jane, and myself —
then walked into the store. We went to the back room. Jane went
to put her dress in the bathroom as I was going into the office.
This is when I noticed the office was out of order. Drawers were
open and papers were all messed up. I then told Jane to come here
and we called for Martie to come to the door. Martie went into
the office to check and make sure Robert's checkbook was there.
We went out of the office and I noticed that the back door was
unlocked. I told both Jane and Martie that the door was locked.
We then went to check on the money. Seeing that the rugs were
messed up, we didn't touch anything. We went to the front of
the store to call Robert. He was already on his way to the store.
When Robert arrived about 8:05 we told him what happened.
He then looked it over himself and he called the police officer.

Susan _____

4-30-20__

Appendix E

Chapter 5:
Pressure/Motive: Company B

Exercise 1: Explain the utilization of "I appreciate that" and " I am trying to understand" in Inquiry 46. Identify terminology an interviewer should avoid at this point within an interview dealing with the resume. Give three examples of how Inquiry 46 could have been made in a manner that would minimize the possibility of a negative outcome.

Subject: Of course it was court-ordered that I had got back on the medication. And so I was on medication at that time. I don't know from the standpoint of what did it change. Why did I stop taking it? I usually do though start thinking about "Why do I need this?" And again, at the time that the crime was committed I had pulled myself off the medication. But that is no excuse. I don't want to use that as an excuse.

Interviewing Inquiry 46

Interviewer: I appreciate that. I am just saying, I am trying to understand at the point where you begin to fabricate your resume—to be deceptive on your resume.

Exercise 2: Explain what the interviewee reveals about himself when he remarks, "And so I fabricated it in order to be at a level of income that I thought I should be at."

Subject: Exactly. That's a good point. I had to have work. Trying to make some kind of income. I did not ... the level of income I had been able to make ... I didn't see me ever being able to make that kind of income if I had went and just basically told someone,

"This is my past, this is what I have done, are you going to give me a chance?" And so I fabricated it in order to be at a level of income that I thought I should be at.

Exercise 3: Explain the interviewee's use of the words "thought" and should."

Subject: Exactly. That's a good point. I had to have work. Trying to make some kind of income. I did not ... the level of income I had been able to make ... I didn't see me ever being able to make that kind of income if I had went and just basically told someone' "This is my past, this is what I have done, are you going to give me a chance?" And so I fabricated it in order to be at a level of income that I thought I should be at.

Exercise 4: Link both "thought" and "should" to the rationalization process as previously addressed in Exercise 3.

Application Question 1: The interviewee has revealed significant information in his utilization of an aside as he responds to Inquiry 48. Exactly what has the interviewee revealed to the attentive interviewer?

Interviewing Inquiry 48

Interviewer: Did you go into the door with Company B with the idea, "I am going to do right while I am here?"

Subject: Absolutely. I gone through this in my life in the past thinking "Okay, what I done in the past is the past and I am going to go in here and do the best job that I can do." And that was my total intention at the time. I had no intention of ever doing anything wrong in the company.

Exercise 5: Read the interviewee's response to Inquiry 49 once again. Down the side of a sheet of paper make a list of the pronouns used by the interviewee. Explain what the pronoun utilization discloses to the attentive interviewer.

Interviewing Inquiry 49

Interviewer: Okay. Day one—Company B—false resume, here's your office (you now have the job under a false resume). Take me from there.

Subject: Okay. Basically the company was a small, family-owned company here in town. And that is a lot of the reason why they did not do a lot of background checks. But the gentleman that had come in—they hired a new president and the board of directors at that time—was ready for the company to take the next step and start growing. And I had a big part in that. We did. We took the company from, when I went into, the day I was employed the balance sheet-income statement was about 5.7 million a year was the revenue. When I left it was thirty-eight to forty-two; was going to be in that range. We had taken a very small revenued (*sic*) company up to being a very big revenued company in just a short period of time that we were there.

Exercise 6: Read the interviewee's response to Inquiry 54. Once more on a sheet of paper make a list of the pronouns used by the interviewee. Explain the changes in the pronoun use by the interviewee in response to Inquiry 54 in comparison to his pronoun use in his response to Inquiry 49. Explain why the frequent usage of the third person pronoun "they" is important for the interviewer to note.

Interviewing Inquiry 54

Interviewer: Tell me about that.

Subject: They—I am going to throw some numbers around so that people can see the relationship and a little bit about why I felt the way that I did. The president was at 250,000 plus. That was his salary. At that time as a VP, I was making 65. And at his death—well the company due to all the things that I and the president—we had had several board meetings, we had been to various cities and states doing presentations. Well, they thought that they were going to give me the position. And you can imagine at that point I knew what he made and I knew what I made. I thought, "This is going to be a great opportunity for me." Well they bring me into a meeting with the board and they give me a $15,000 raise and tell me that I am going to run the company. And I get—not upset but I was upset. I thought a little bit, "The audacity." And this goes in a little bit—you have to know some of the background—the reason why the revenue had gone up quite a bit—I really thought was primarily the work that I and the quality control director had done at that plant. And what we had done; we had got them from being a mom and pop 'til we started doing government contracts. And so we started producing loads and loads of product for the government, which took the revenue straight up. Now it wasn't the most profitable so you didn't see such an increase in income but you did see the revenue change and product flowing through there. Our price point on all the raw materials was going down because we were able to buy in quantity. And so the company had really got a whole lot better and I really thought I deserved, at that point, more income level than going from where he was—from sixty-five to eighty. Now that's what started permeating me having some ill will toward the company.

Exercise 7: Diagram the fraud triangle with the terminology utilized by the interviewee in his response to Inquiry 55 as it relates to pressure/motive. Explain the pressure/motive element as articulated by the interviewee.

Interviewing Inquiry 55

Interviewer: I see.

Subject: And at that point—it's totally different from the crime the first time. I [was] feeling like they owed me more money than they were paying me. And so there was opportunity and so I started myself again, cutting checks to myself. And not to the level that I did at Company A. These were just small checks and basically trying to get myself compensated to the level I thought I should be compensated at.

Exercise 8: Summarize the lessons learned from the inquiries made and the responses given by the interviewee in Inquiries 42–55.

Interviewing Inquiry 42

Interviewer: Tell me what happened from the point—probation, no prison time—to the present.

Subject: Okay. Of course there are certain skills that I have in my life and then of course I started looking for other work. And I was sending out resumes. And that's when I got introduced to Company B. Interviewed with the president of the company who had had years and years of experience in the industry but he again—it was a brand-new small—not a brand-new, an old company that was ready to take the next step and start growing. Went in, interviewed with him, second day he called me back for an interview and hired me. This is where I think a lot of people need more things too. And I know I put them in place in the business that I am in now is background checks. If they had done a background check on me prior to hiring they would have never put themselves in the situation where I perpetrated in Company B.

Interviewing Inquiry 43

Interviewer: So, in Company B you're going in the door as what?

Subject: As basically a resume that was doctored and interviewing and I went in as a controller.

Interviewing Inquiry 44

Interviewer: Tell me how you doctored your resume.

Subject: I just basically made up for the time of not including company A in the resume. I just extended the time that I was with another company.

Interviewing Inquiry 45

Interviewer: At the time when you put together that resume and you were looking for employment, where are we as far as the bipolar issue?

Subject: Of course it was court-ordered that I had got back on the medication. And so I was on medication at that time. I don't know from the standpoint of what did it change. Why did I stop taking it? I usually do though start thinking, "Why do I need this?" And again, at the time that the crime was committed I had pulled myself off the medication. But that is no excuse. I don't want to use that as an excuse.

Interviewing Inquiry 46

Interviewer: I appreciate that. I am just saying, I am trying to understand at the point where you begin to fabricate your resume—to be deceptive on your resume.

Interviewing Inquiry 47

Interviewer: I understand. But (your) coming in the door was under a false flag, as it were.

Subject: Yes.

Interviewing Inquiry 48

Interviewer: Did you go into the door with Company B with the idea, "I am going to do right while I am here"?

Subject: Absolutely. I gone through this in my life in the past thinking "Okay, what I done in the past is the past and I am going to go in here and do the best job that I can do." And that was my total intention at the time. I had no intention of ever doing anything wrong in the company.

Interviewing Inquiry 49

Interviewer: Okay. Day one—Company B—false resume, here's your office (you now have the job under a false resume). Take me from there.

Subject: Okay. Basically the company was a small, family-owned company here in town. And that is a lot of the reason why they did not do a lot of background checks. But the gentleman that had come in—they hired a new president and the board of directors at that time—was ready for the company to take the next step and start growing. And I had a big part in that. We did. We took the company from — when I went into — the day I was employed the balance sheet-income statement was about 5.7 million a year was the revenue. When I left it was thirty-eight to forty-two was going to be in that range. We had taken a very small revenued (*sic*) company up to being a very big revenued company in just a short period of time that we were there.

Interviewing Inquiry 50

Interviewer: That was over six times.

Subject: Absolutely as far as revenue. Now the income did not go up six times.

Interviewing Inquiry 51

Interviewer: Tell me about the work schedule. You come in there; you are bound and determined to work hard. How many hours did you work with that company?

Subject: It was a lot of hours. We started early in the morning, left late at night for the first eight to ten months. We were really busy. Probably sixty-five to seventy hour work weeks, I think what it was. Growing, growing — actually throughout my tenure — while the president was still living; I mean I got a promotion to being controller being VP. I was actually put on; basically made an officer of the company. And again, doing really well, the company is really growing. Really busy trying to put systems in. All the good stuff that was supposed to be going on.

Interviewing Inquiry 52

Interviewer: When you got promoted, did the president leave?

Subject: No, actually the president passed away.

Interviewing Inquiry 53

Interviewer: Did someone move up into his place?

Subject: That was a big part to where the problem comes in.

Interviewing Inquiry 54

Interviewer: Tell me about that.

Subject: They — I am going to throw some numbers around so that people can see the relationship and a little bit about why I felt the way that I did. The president was at 250,000 plus. That was his salary. At that time as a VP, I was making sixty-five. And at his death — well the company due to all the things that I and the president — we had had several board meetings, we had been to various cities and states doing presentations. Well, they thought that they were going to give me the position. And you can imagine at that point I knew what he made and I knew what I made. I thought, "This is going to be a great opportunity for me." Well they bring me into a meeting with the board and they give me a $15,000 raise and tell me that I am going to run the company. And I get — not upset but I was upset. I thought a little bit, "The audacity." And this goes in a little bit — you have to know some of the background; the reason why the revenue had gone up quite a bit — I really thought was primarily the work that I and the quality control director had done at that plant. And what we had done — we had got them from being a mom and pop 'til we started doing government contracts. And so we started producing loads and loads of product for the government which took the revenue straight up. Now it wasn't the most profitable so you didn't see such an increase in income but you did see the revenue change and product flowing through there. Our price point on all the raw materials was going down because we were able to buy in quantity. And so the company had really got a whole lot better and I really thought I deserved, at that point, more income level than going from where he was — from sixty-five to eighty. Now that's what started permeating me having some ill will toward the company.

Interviewing Inquiry 55

Interviewer: I see.

Subject: And at that point; it's totally different from the crime the first time. I feeling like they owed me more money than they were paying me. And so there was opportunity and so I started myself again, cutting checks to myself. And not to the level that I did at Company A. These were just small checks and basically trying to get myself compensated to the level I thought I should be compensated at.

Appendix F

Chapter 6:
Opportunity: Company B

Exercise 1: Diagram the fraud triangle with the terminology utilized by the interviewee in the subject's response to Inquiry 56 as it relates to opportunity. Explain the opportunity element as articulated by the interviewee.

Interviewing Inquiry 56

Interviewer: I see.

Subject: And at that point [the commission of fraud at Company B] — it's totally different from the crime the first time. I was feeling like they owed me more money than they were paying me. And so there was opportunity and so I started myself again, cutting checks to myself. And not to the level that I did at Company A. These were just small checks and basically trying to get myself compensated to the level I thought I should be compensated at.

Exercise 2: Explain how the interviewee avoids the implication of guilt in the statement, "So in your mind, you were just making things right."

Interviewing Inquiry 57

Interviewer: So in your mind, you were just making things right.

Subject: Yes, but that is a manic-depressive mind.

Exercise 3: Explain how the interviewer's summarization of the interviewee's mindset at the time of the commission of the fraud is important to the overall positive outcome of the interview.

Interviewing Inquiry 58

Interviewer: I understand. I am just saying, your mind at that particular time — as you say — you got the promotion, but you didn't get the compensation you felt was suitable for somebody taking on that much responsibility.

Subject: Yes sir.

Application Question 1: What does the interviewee's frequent use of the pronoun "they" in the following narrative indicate to you?

Subject: During that meeting when they gave me the raise we had a confrontation right there. The guy — no matter how strong the board of directors are, there is always a couple that are going to be leading the pack. And the two that were leading the pack at that point basically were argumentative with me. They said, "Well this guy had so many years of experience." I said, "Well I don't care — I mean, I know you guys are looking in thinking what this gentleman was doing but let me tell you the real story of how we have been going and how we have been doing and how we're getting there." And ... and so but it didn't work. They said, "If you are not satisfied with that, we'll go out and hire a president to come in and you can work for him or her."

Application Question 2: How would you incorporate the use of the word "they" into the conduct of the interview from this point forward?

Subject: During that meeting when they gave me the raise we had a confrontation right there. The guy — no matter how strong the board of directors are, there is always a couple that are going to be leading the pack. And the two that were leading the pack at that point basically were argumentative with me. They said, "Well this guy had so many years of experience." I said, "Well I don't care — I mean, I know you guys are looking in thinking what this gentleman was doing but let me tell you the real story of how we have been going and how we have been doing and how we're getting there." And ... and so but it didn't work. They said, "If you are not satisfied with that, we'll go out and hire a president to come in and you can work for."

Exercise 4: In Inquiry 61 the interviewer has summarized the situation as articulated by the interviewee. Write a summary of the interviewee's narrative with regard to Company B in your own words. Read your summary out loud as if you were speaking to the interviewee. Honestly critique yourself on how it sounded to you as you were reading it out loud. Make any changes to your summary that would enhance its effectiveness. Read it out loud again. Repeat until you feel you have it right.

Interviewing Inquiry 61

Interviewer: At this point you were placed in the dilemma wherein you could stay where you were at your current salary and work for somebody else or you could take the promotion at the salary that was nowhere near what you felt like you should be making.

Subject: Yes sir.

Application Question 3: As the interviewer in a fraud-related interview, how would you adjust the conduct of your interview after having picked up on this repeated use of the pronoun "we"?

Subject: No. I was basically working pretty hard at that point. What we had to do at the ... the part that I was missing on my resume to be able to take the company where we were going—the first thing that I did and that's what the board actually said is probably one of my biggest strengths was putting the right people in the right place to actually make me look good and everybody else look good. So the first thing I did I had to go out and get a marketing person. Because if we were going to continue to grow at the pace that we did—I had no marketing or sales background at that point. I had to have a marketing salesperson. So I went out and actually I put an ad in the paper and we finally found someone who was excellent and he is running the company today. That was totally qualified to do it. Literally—and this always shocks everyone—his salary was going to be $20,000 more a year than mine was. And I was hiring him to work for me because that was what he was going to demand. That's what his skill set demanded. And so we hired him on as marketing salesperson making more money than I was at that time.

Application Question 4: What effect do you think hiring someone at $20,000 more than him would have on the interviewee's inter-action with opportunity?

Subject: No. I was basically working pretty hard at that point. What we had to do at the ... the part that I was missing on my resume to be able to take the company where we were going — the first thing that I did and that's what the board actually said is probably one of my biggest strengths was putting the right people in the right place to actually make me look good and everybody else look good. So the first thing I did I had to go out and get a marketing person.

Because if we were going to continue to grow at the pace that we did — I had no marketing-sales background at that point. I had to have a marketing salesperson. So I went out and actually I put an ad in the paper and we finally found someone who was excel-lent and he is running the company today. That was totally quali-fied to do it.   Literally — and this always shocks everyone — his salary was going to be $20,000 more a year than mine was. And I was hiring him to work for me because that was what he was going to demand. That's what his skill set demanded. And so we hired him on as marketing-salesperson making more money than I was at that time.

Application Question 5: If a revelation ($20,000 difference in salary) to this effect were to arise during the conduct of your interviews, how would you apply this information in the conduct of the fraud-related interview?

Application Question 6: If another reader of this text were to re-spond to the preceding question with, "I would not incorporate this information into my interview," how would you respond to them?

Application Question 7: How else could you make the point in In-quiry 65?

Interviewing Inquiry 65

Interviewer: And I don't doubt it but I just find it interesting they took your word when you said he deserved more money but they didn't take your word when you said you deserved more money.

Exercise 5: Review Inquiries 56–65 once again. On a sheet of paper, list all of the instances when the interviewee answered in the affirmative. Explain the advantage for the interviewer capable of maneuvering the interviewee into answering in the affirmative.

Interviewing Inquiry 56

Interviewer: I see.

Subject: And at that point—it's totally different from the crime the first time. I was feeling like they owed me more money than they were paying me. And so there was opportunity and so I started myself again, cutting checks to myself. And not to the level that I did at Company A. These were just small checks and basically trying to get myself compensated to the level I thought I should be compensated at.

Interviewing Inquiry 57

Interviewer: So in your mind, you were just making things right.

Subject: Yes, but that is a manic-depressive mind.

Interviewing Inquiry 58

Interviewer: I understand. I am just saying, your mind at that particular time—as you say—you got the promotion, but you didn't get the compensation you felt was suitable for somebody taking on that much responsibility.

Subject: Yes sir.

Interviewing Inquiry 59

Interviewer: Did you ever say to somebody, "You know, I think I deserve more money"?

Subject: Yes sir.

Interviewing Inquiry 60

Interviewer: Tell me about that.

Subject: During that meeting when they gave me the raise we had a confrontation right there. The guy—no matter how strong the board of directors are, there is always a couple that are going to be leading the pack. And the two that were leading the pack at that point basically were argumentative with me. They said, "Well this guy had so many years of experience." I said, "Well I don't care—I mean, I know you guys are looking in thinking what this gentleman was doing but let me tell you the real story of how we have been going and how we have been doing and how we're getting there." And ... and so but it didn't work. They said, "If you are not satisfied with that, we'll go out and hire a president to come in and you can work for."

Interviewing Inquiry 61

Interviewer: At this point you were placed in the dilemma wherein you could stay where you were at your current salary and work for somebody else or you could take the promotion at the salary that was nowhere near what you felt like you should be making.

Subject: Yes sir.

Interviewing Inquiry 62

Interviewer: During this same time were there any of these expenditures as far as the material aspects that you were talking about; are you buying a lot of fancy stuff, buying new cars living the high life or are you just working hard?

Subject: No. I was basically working pretty hard at that point. What we had to do at the ... the part that I was missing on my resume to be able to take the company where we were going—the first thing that I did and that's what the board actually said is probably one of my biggest strengths was putting the right people in the right place to actually make me look good and everybody else look good. So the first thing I did I had to go out and get a marketing person. Because if we were going to continue to grow at the pace that we did—I had no marketing-sales background at that point. I had to have a marketing salesperson. So I went out and actually I put an ad in the paper and we finally found someone who was excellent and he is running the company today. That was totally qualified to do it. Literally—and this always shocks everyone—his salary was going to be $20,000 more a year than mine was. And I was hiring him to work for me because that was what he was going to demand. That's what his skill set demanded. And so we hired him on as marketing-salesperson making more money than I was at that time.

Interviewing Inquiry 63

Interviewer: And the board of directors approved you hiring somebody at a salary that was 20,000 more than you and that person (with the higher salary) was answering to you?

Subject: Yes sir.

Interviewing Inquiry 64

Interviewer: They didn't say ...

Subject: Oh they asked me, "Why? What is your rational behind this?" I said, "I think the guy is worth this. This is his past salary range that he has been in. This is the company; the history that he has with other companies." I told them, "This is the right guy for the job." And it has proved out that I was right about that. He was extremely qualified to do the job.

Interviewing Inquiry 65

Interviewer: And I don't doubt it but I just find it interesting they took your word when you said he deserved more money but they didn't take your word when you said you deserved more money.

Subject: Right.

Exercise 6: Read the following.

A 41-year-old woman has been charged with taking $30,000. It has been reported that she made unauthorized credit card purchases and wrote company checks to herself to carry out the embezzlement.

You are responsible for conducting the interview. In the development of your interview plan, address the following:

- What documentation would you have on hand during the conduct of the interview?
- What could the documentation possibly inform you of with regard to pressure/motive?

Exercise 7: Summarize the lessons learned from the inquiries made and the responses given by the interviewee in Inquiries 56–65.

Interviewing Inquiry 56

Interviewer: I see.

Subject: And at that point—it's totally different from the crime the first time. I was feeling like they owed me more money than they were paying me. And so there was opportunity and so I started myself again, cutting checks to myself. And not to the level that I did at Company A. These were just small checks and basically trying to get myself compensated to the level I thought I should be compensated at.

Interviewing Inquiry 57

Interviewer: So in your mind, you were just making things right.

Subject: Yes, but that is a manic-depressive mind.

Interviewing Inquiry 58

Interviewer: I understand. I am just saying, your mind at that particular time—as you say—you got the promotion, but you didn't get the compensation you felt was suitable for somebody taking on that much responsibility.

Subject: Yes sir.

Interviewing Inquiry 59

Interviewer: Did you ever say to somebody, "You know, I think I deserve more money"?

Subject: Yes sir.

Interviewing Inquiry 60

Interviewer: Tell me about that.

Subject: During that meeting when they gave me the raise we had a confrontation right there. The guy—no matter how strong the board of directors are, there is always a couple that are going to be leading the pack. And the two that were leading the pack at that point basically were argumentative with me. They said, "Well this guy had so many years of experience." I said, "Well I don't care— I mean, I know you guys are looking in thinking what this gentleman was doing but let me tell you the real story of how we have been going and how we have been doing and how we're getting there." And ... and so but it didn't work. They said, "If you are not satisfied with that, we'll go out and hire a president to come in and you can work for."

Interviewing Inquiry 61

Interviewer: At this point you were placed in the dilemma wherein you could stay where you were at your current salary and work for somebody else or you could take the promotion at the salary that was nowhere near what you felt like you should be making?

Subject: Yes sir.

Interviewing Inquiry 62

Interviewer: During this same time were there any of these expenditures as far as the material aspects that you were talking about; are you buying a lot of fancy stuff, buying new cars living the high life or are you just working hard?

Subject: No. I was basically working pretty hard at that point. What we had to do at the ... the part that I was missing on my resume to be able to take the company where we were going—the first thing that I did and that's what the board actually said is probably one of my biggest strengths was putting the right people in the right place to actually make me look good and everybody else look good. So the first thing I did I had to go out and get a marketing person. Because if we were going to continue to grow at the pace that we did—I had no marketing-sales background at that point. I had to have a marketing salesperson. So I went out and actually I put an ad in the paper and we finally found someone who was excellent and he is running the company today. That was totally qualified to do it. Literally—and this always shocks everyone—his salary was going to be $20,000 more a year than mine was. And I was hiring him to work for me because that was what he was going to demand. That's what his skill set demanded. And so we hired him on as marketing-salesperson making more money than I was at that time.

Interviewing Inquiry 63

Interviewer: And the board of directors approved you hiring somebody at a salary that was 20,000 more than you and that person (with the higher salary) was answering to you?

Subject: Yes sir.

Interviewing Inquiry 64

Interviewer: They didn't say …

Subject: Oh they asked me, "Why? What is your rational behind this?" I said, "I think the guy is worth this. This is his past salary range that he has been in. This is the company; the history that he has with other companies." I told them, "This is the right guy for the job." And it has proved out that I was right about that. He was extremely qualified to do the job.

Interviewing Inquiry 65

Interviewer: And I don't doubt it but I just find it interesting they took your word when you said he deserved more money but they didn't take your word when you said you deserved more money.

Subject: Right.

Appendix G

Chapter 7: Rationalization: Company B

Application Question 1: Think of a significant situation wherein you felt that you had been treated unfairly. What was your first response?

Application Question 2: Did it cross your mind to respond by doing something that would either get back at someone or serve, in your mind, to make things right?

Application Question 3: By reflecting on your own response in a given situation, can you better understand (but not necessarily agree with) how an individual may react to their own situation by committing fraud?

Exercise 1: Diagram the fraud triangle with the terminology utilized by the interviewee in his response to Inquiry 66 as it relates to rationalization. Explain the rationalization element as articulated by the interviewee.

Interviewing Inquiry 66

Interviewer: Certainly that [the board of directors approving a higher salary for a subordinate] had to produce a certain amount of angst in you.

Subject: It did. It did. It created a lot of anxiety in me and about those times too, the funds that I started funneling to myself started about the time that the anxiety got pretty heavy.

Exercise 2: Note the highlighted terms and phrases in this reading of the interviewee's response to Inquiry 84.

Subject: Oh it was a *nerve wracking period of time*—for me it was. Because at that point it was like in June that they did the six month audit. And there hadn't been a lot of funds taken at that point. It was just very, very little. And I was *a nervous wreck literally.* But they came in, did all the checks and balances that a midterm audit was supposed to be doing. And then *they never asked any questions.* They ... I don't know that they just didn't pull the right checks to check. Because they would go through and pick certain checks and then do and audit. Do a test, what they called them and never caught anything that was out of kilter at that time, even though there had been some crime already committed.

Connect the first two highlighted phrases with the third explaining the advantages and cautions for the interviewer.

Exercise 3: In the interviewee's response to Inquiry 87 he states that he "was angry with them," "part of it was justification for what I was doing," and "at the same time I was a nervous wreck." Explain how these stated emotions and rationales can be woven together by the interviewer to carry the interview forward to a productive conclusion.

Interviewing Inquiry 87

Interviewer: How were you feeling when they were interviewing you and asking you those questions?

Subject: It was a miserable time for me because I ... at that period of time ... I was still ... I was angry with them and really thought it ... part of it was justification for what I was doing. But at the same time I was a nervous wreck. I knew that if I ever got in trouble again because I had the first crime that I had committed. Basically what they had done with that was to listen to the judge. He said he was going to put this in a drawer and leave it there. And if I never ever did anything wrong again it would stay in a drawer. But I knew if I ever got caught doing something like that again ... In the back of my mind I don't know why I did it. But if I got caught I knew I was going to get in very, very serious trouble.

Exercise 4: Read the following.

A 41-year-old woman has been charged with taking $30,000. It has been reported that she made unauthorized credit card purchases and wrote company checks to herself to carry out the embezzlement.

You are responsible for conducting the interview. In your preparation consider the following:

- What documentary evidence will you have in hand prior to conducting the interview?
- How will you plan to utilize the documentary evidence during the conduct of the interview?
- When will you present the documentary evidence during the conduct of the interview?

Exercise 5: Summarize the lessons learned from the inquiries and the responses in Inquiries 66–106.

Interviewing Inquiry 66

Interviewer: Certainly that had to produce a certain amount of angst in you.

Subject: It did. It did. It created a lot of anxiety in me and about those times too, the funds that I started funneling to myself started about the time that the anxiety got pretty heavy.

Interviewing Inquiry 67

Interviewer: Looking back, do you think the fact that, not only your inequity as far as your pay but the disparity between what someone that works for you was making and what you were making—do you see that as a precursor that began to cause you to do that?

Subject: Do I think ... you know I have answered that question a million times lying around at night. If I had brought him in at a lower rate—did that push me over—do I think I still would have if they had not done anything about adjusting my salary? Do I think I would have still tried to funnel funds to myself? And the answer to that is, yes. Now the gentleman that I hired making more was a thorn in my flesh but I really at that time … and not only did I hire him at a certain salary—but at the time too he had some personal medical bills that was associated with a child of his that I didn't ask for an approval [for payment]—but it was like somewhere between 17–20,000 and I cut a check and helped him so that we could get him on board. That was how important I knew that this gentleman was going to be to the future success of the company.

Interviewing Inquiry 68

Interviewer: You labeled him as "a thorn in your flesh." Are you talking about the salary or him as an individual?

Subject: No. Him as an individual was wonderful. No. Nothing that this gentleman ever did or said or anything was negative toward me. He supported me. Even though I think he probably sat over thinking he was probably more qualified for my job than I was from the standpoint of having the whole gamut of responsibility. From the financial side, he had no knowledge, he was not an accountant. As so I think that's where he … but he did his job well.

We continued to grow the company. We had new accounts coming on board due to this gentleman. The thorn was not him it was that he was actually making more money than I was.

Interviewing Inquiry 69

Interviewer: Was he appreciative of the fact that you signed a check for 17,000?

Subject: Very. Extremely I think he was.

Interviewing Inquiry 70

Interviewer: You said the checks that you were starting to write now were smaller checks.

Subject: Right.

Interviewing Inquiry 71

Interviewer: But were there more of them?

Subject: Yes sir.

Interviewing Inquiry 72

Interviewer: Tell me about that.

Subject: Okay. The amount ... the total amount—and this gets into a very hard subject for me—because the money ... and I am going to say this and then we'll go back to that if you don't mind. The money that I am literally paying them back is not literally the funds ... the checks that I wrote. I mean because ... now this gets into another situation where I was in a relationship. The money I am paying back is actually the expense stuff that was the credit card; traveling and all that stuff that they said were not approved. When I was arrested it was $34,000 and that is what I am still paying back to them. Now the $117,000 that over the nine months that I was writing myself checks ... not nine months ... May–December ... seven months. The money that I wrote ... that was in little, small, little bitty checks ... I mean 5,000 here, 7,000 there. That's how I did. I didn't write any $25,000 checks to myself or along those lines.

Interviewing Inquiry 73

Interviewer: Within Company B was there a system of checks and balances or could you just sign a check?

Subject: No. I could period. My signature was it. Which was crazy.

Interviewing Inquiry 74

Interviewer: Was there any type of audit review or checks and balances as you say?

Subject: The lady that did the work for me did the reconciliation. Now I do think that this lady ... she had been with the company about twelve to fifteen years. I can't remember the exact number. She had been with the company a long time. I do think that she suspicioned (sic) the checks that she was reconciling going in but she went on with it. She never did bring it to my attention or to my knowledge [never] brought it outside to the company's attention.

Interviewing Inquiry 75

Interviewer: While all of this was going on did you have some indication that she had some suspicion?

Subject: A little bit.

Interviewing Inquiry 76

Interviewer: What specifically was going on that made you think she had a suspicion?

Subject: Because I knew how good she was. And I know how loyal she was to the company. I just felt ... I don't know what it was ... I can still feel it today that she felt an uneasiness about what she was doing.

Interviewing Inquiry 77

Interviewer: When you were communicating?

Subject: Yes sir. And when ... you know, when the reconciliation— she'd bring the reconciliation to me and all the checks and everything. Because I required all the accounts and the general ledger to be reconciled at month's end. And it was just a funny feeling I had. I thought that she had some, you know, knowledge of what was going on.

Interviewing Inquiry 78

Interviewer: Okay.

Subject: Now after the fact she really did, I think, from the standpoint of what I know.

Interviewing Inquiry 79

Interviewer: What caused this house of cards to come down?

Subject: I guess from the standpoint of ... there was an audit required. They came in and ... we were using a very low ... I guess ... low-powered accounting system. And there had become some is-sues the balance sheet and the income statements and those kind of things. So they actually came in and were trying to reconcile the accounts. And so the external auditors actually caught that I had ac-tually done something. They started questioning some of the checks being written.

Interviewing Inquiry 80

Interviewer: You said there were some issues which came up that caused this audit to occur.

This is not something that happened on a regular basis?

Subject: Yes sir?

Interviewing Inquiry 81

Interviewer: This is not something that happened on a regular basis as far as this audit if I am understanding you correctly.

Subject: Well they were supposed ... they were doing ... every six months they were doing an internal audit. And actually one of them ... I had actually passed through the internal audit after ... after some stuff had been done.

Interviewing Inquiry 82

Interviewer: Okay. Let's talk about that.

Subject: Okay.

Interviewing Inquiry 83

Interviewer: You are already doing "some stuff" as you say and you are passing through this audit. This is the time when the auditor is there with you within that division.

Subject: Yes sir.

Interviewing Inquiry 84

Interviewer: Tell me about that time.

Subject: Oh it was a nerve-wracking period of time—for me it was. Because at that point it was like in June that they did the six-month audit. And there hadn't been a lot of funds taken at that point. It was just very, very little. And I was a nervous wreck literally. But they came in, did all the checks and balances that a midterm audit was supposed to be doing. And then they never asked any questions. They … I don't know that they just didn't pull the right checks to check. Because they would go through and pick certain checks and then do and audit. Do a test, what they called them and never caught anything that was out of kilter at that time, even though there had been some crime already committed.

Interviewing Inquiry 85

Interviewer: No one interviewed you? No one sat down and talked with you? They just did the audit?

Subject: Yeah, they just came in. They came in and performed a mechanical audit. Of course they interviewed me. They had to ask me questions about this and ask questions about that.

Interviewing Inquiry 86

Interviewer: Tell me about the interview.

Subject: From the audit standpoint they did ask the typical questions: "Is there anything going on within the company that we need to know about?" Of course they did a balance sheet-income statement audit. And they were going through and reconciling all of the reconciliations that had been done. And so the accounts reconciled the balance sheet. All they did was test work and we passed that audit.

Interviewing Inquiry 87

Interviewer: How were you feeling when they were interviewing you and asking you those questions?

Subject: It was a miserable time for me because I ... at that period of time ... I was still ... I was angry with them and really thought it ... part of it was justification for what I was doing. But at the same time I was a nervous wreck. I knew that if I ever got in trouble again because I had the first crime that I had committed. Basically what they had done with that was to listen to the judge. He said he was going to put this in a drawer and leave it there. And if I never ever did anything wrong again it would stay in a drawer. But I knew if I ever got caught doing something like that again ... In the back of my mind I don't know why I did it. But if I got caught I knew I was going to get in very, very serious trouble.

Interviewing Inquiry 88

Interviewer: During the time that the auditor was interviewing you and talking to you did it ever cross your mind, "Do they know something?"

Subject: During the first audit?

Interviewing Inquiry 89

Interviewer: Yes.

Subject: No. Not at all. I did not ... because the amounts were so small at that time—we are talking from the first of May 'til June, Okay? I just really didn't think that the size of that coming about was going to be found. Because it just wouldn't have raised a flag. The amounts were so small.

Interviewing Inquiry 90

Interviewer: If they had randomly pulled one of your checks and placed it on the table, what would have happened?

Subject: Uh … I don't know what I would have done.

Interviewing Inquiry 91

Interviewer: Let's imagine that was the case.

Subject: Okay.

Interviewing Inquiry 92

Interviewer: And I am saying, "David, can you tell me about this check for $5,000?"

Subject: There would have been no way I would have had an answer. I would have said, "No, I can't tell you about it."

Interviewing Inquiry 93

Interviewer: Okay.

Subject: And we would have gone from there. See that's the stupidity about it. Because if you think about … if they had of pulled that check … I would have had no answer. Now, knowing what I would have known at that time, I would probably have come up with something. I don't know if you would call it BS but I would have tried to BS my way through what it represented. But I don't know from that point what I would have done.

Interviewing Inquiry 94

Interviewer: Let's say you were able to BS your way through that first check.

Subject: Yeah

Interviewing Inquiry 95

Interviewer: And then they pull another check.

Subject: Yeah.

Interviewing Inquiry 96

Interviewer: I know you hadn't written a lot by the time of the first audit but would you have tried to do it again?

Subject: I would have tried my best to have gotten through that.

Interviewing Inquiry 97

Interviewer: Let's say there were three or four of them.

Subject: No. I think if they had of found that it would have been over.

Interviewing Inquiry 98

Interviewer: That would have done it?

Subject: Yeah. Because the external audit company that was doing the auditing for us was a very reputable company. And if they would have found some impropriety they would have blown it all up. I really do think that.

Interviewing Inquiry 99

Interviewer: David, you are obviously a nice guy. I can tell you are a nice guy. And you did not commit a crime that involved much in the way of sophistication. You wrote checks to yourself and you deposited them in your own account.

Subject: It was so simple that is probably why it slipped through. But at the same time, the proper checks and balances put in would have stopped any of this. I should not ... as president of the company I should not have check-signing authority. I should not have the authority without some kind of checks and balances of someone else having to sign that check with me that reports not directly to me. Because even if I had a second person, I could have taken the check in and said, "Sign this. We have got to do this."

Interviewing Inquiry 100

Interviewer: Okay.

Subject: And most likely they would have done it. See you need that checks and balances within a company. A president or the controller of the company has no business signing checks for that company.

Interviewing Inquiry 101

Interviewer: So if you were going to help a company put in a proactive policy and procedure those would be some of the things you would have in your policy and procedure—that the auditor would ensure this is not happening among other things?

Subject: Absolutely. Yes exactly

Interviewing Inquiry 102

Interviewer: In looking back—I mean we are all human. As the Bible says, "We have all fallen short."

Subject: Yes.

Interviewing Inquiry 103

Interviewer: If you look back and said, "If I was going to do something wrong again." and I believe that you don't want to do that.

Subject: Never again.

Interviewing Inquiry 104

Interviewer: Have you ever thought, "This is how I would do it in a manner that was more sophisticated?"

Subject: You are going down that route that people that do it get into. There is no way that someone is not going to get caught.

Interviewing Inquiry 105

Interviewer: You think?

Subject: I do not think that anybody, long term, is going to get away with it. Eventually they are either going to get caught up in it their own self — do something that someone is going to see wrong — or companies ... the accounting systems that are in ... balances that are in are going to eventually catch someone. I don't think anyone is smart enough ever to propriate (*sic*) a crime and continue propriating (*sic*) it and not eventually get caught. I don't ... I don't think there is anything I can go back and say, "Okay. If I had done this, this would not have happened." You have to imagine during those eight months in jail, I went through those things: "Why did I do this? Why did I do that?" Because it was so stupid! I mean I could have done this different. I would have done that different. But it is really not about that. The healing process that I went through was about saying "Nothing you can do is going to keep you from getting caught. You are eventually going to get caught."

Interviewing Inquiry 106

Interviewer: While you are with Company B and once you get past the initial audit. Every day you get up and look in the mirror, you shave and do you think to yourself, "I am a thief"? Do you think to yourself, "If they had treated me right in the first place this would not have been necessary"? What do you think during the course of your day?

Subject: I do think sometimes ... but not now ... I did. I have gone through a lot of healing. And I have done a lot of mind searching. I don't think that anything justifies what I did. I agreed to a salary ... agreed to a job. This is what the requirements are, you do it. Now that is where I am at with that attitude about they owed me more money. I agreed to the salary. When I look at my resume that is all that resume demanded on the market. All I could have made. For me thinking that a guy with three years experience in this industry should be making the $250,000 that that guy having twenty-five years in that industry was making was ludicrous. Now should there have been a happy medium? In my head I think there should have been a happy medium. But it doesn't justify what I did.